About this book

This book contains ecological field studies techniques, that can be conducted in wild nature by non-professional researchers - school and university students together with their teachers, single beginning investigators, families, amateurs of all ages.

The whole book "Field Studies Techniques" includes 5 parts/series corresponding to a specific field sciences (Geography, Botany, Zoology, Hydrobiology and Bioindication) with totally 40 environmental study lessons (see below) covered a wide variety of activities in nature which can be arranged in different seasons of the year. Each series contains techniques focusing on practical skills which can be applied in the field research.

This book promotes a wide variety of outcomes which correspond to established educational standards in many countries. The ecological field study activities address content standards in the areas of earth science, life science, biology and ecology. Intellectual skill development includes questioning, data collection, analysis and drawing conclusions.

This book promotes understanding of ecosystems and the protection of the environment through the training of teachers in specific field study techniques, the education of young people in ecology concepts and issues and the sharing of ecological study results between colleagues. The primary goal of this work is connecting students and teachers, addressing important environmental issues and promoting environmental interest, knowledge and values.

This book is addressed to the middle and secondary level science teachers and students, and for all those who would like to investigate local wild nature, to share ecological and cultural information and work together to help create a better environment.

This specific book "Field Studies Techniques. **Part 4: Hydrobiology and Water Ecology**" is the fourth in the series. Practical skills include the hydrological study of small rivers and streams, physical and chemical properties of natural waters, the study of plankton and benthos, as well as fauna of the spring temporary water reservoirs.

The techniques described in this book, were written by Alexander Bogolyubov (1996-2002), translated into English by Tatiana Tatarinova (2002) and edited by Michael Brody (2003).

The list of all field study lessons:

I. Geography and Landscape Sciences:

Orienteering in the forest

Simple "Eye" Survey of the Field Study Site

Mapping Forest Vegetation

Procedure of the Geological Exposure Description

Studying Minerals and Rocks in Your Area

Plotting a Profile of a River Valley Slope

Simple Procedure of Soil Description

Integrated Study Based on Landscape Profile

Complex Comparative Description of Small Rivers and Streams

Study of Snow Cover Profile

Making a Campfire

II. Botany:

Study of Species Composition and Number of Fungi

Making a Herbarium

The Study of Plants in Your Local Environment

Study of the Vertical Structure of a Forest

Mapping Forest Vegetation

Green Plants Under Snow

Study of the Ecology of Early Flowering Plants

Phenology of Plant Florescence

Assessment of Ecological Features of Meadows on the Base of Vegetation Cover

Assessment of the Vital State of Coniferous Underbrush

Study of Growth Dynamics of Trees Based on Annual Rings

Assessment of the Vital State of a Forest Based on Pine-tree Analysis

Assessment of Environmental State of the Forest Based on Leaves' Asymmetry

III. Zoology:

Study of Forest Invertebrates in the Forest Litter and Wood

Study of Forest Invertebrates in the Grass Layer, Tree Crowns and Air

The Study of Water Invertebrates in a Local River and Assessment of Its Environmental State

Studies of Species Composition and Abundance of Amphibians

Let's Help Birds! (Making Feeders and Nesting Boxes)

Study of Species Composition and Census of Birds Using the Line Transect-counting Method

Studies of Bird Populations Size by Different Methods

Studies of the Day Activity of Singing Birds

Study of Birds' Nesting Life

Methods of Observation of a Chickadee Flock's Territorial Behavior

Procedure of Winter Mammals Route Census by Footprints

Study of Mammal Ecology According to Their Tracks

IV. Hydrobiology and Water Ecology (this book):

Complex Comparative Description of Small Rivers and Streams

Study of Snow Cover Profile

Physical and Chemical Properties of Natural Waters

The Study of Water Invertebrates in a Local River and Assessment of Its Environmental State

Study of Plankton

Study of Fauna of Spring Temporary Water Bodies

Studies of Species Composition and Abundance of Amphibians

V. Bioindication and Nature Monitoring:

Assessment of Air Pollution by Lichen Indication Method

Assessment of the Vital State of a Forest Based on Pine-tree Analysis

Assessment of Ecological Features of Meadows on the Base of Vegetation Cover

Assessment of Environmental State of the Forest Based on Leaves' Asymmetry

Assessment of the Vital State of Coniferous Underbrush

Complex Environmental Assessment of Human Impact on an Area

The Study of Water Invertebrates in a Local River and Assessment of Its Environmental State

Integrated Study Based on Landscape Profile

Study of Growth Dynamics of Trees Based on Annual Rings

If you have any questions or need an advice on the lessons below, write to ecosystema1994@yandex.ru.

____

* **Bold** = important text phrases, ***Bold/Italic*** = key vocabulary, *Italic* = examples and specific illustrations.

Complex comparative description of small rivers and streams

This manual provides a simple scheme of exploring simple hydrological as well as chemical and biological features of a water body. A simple form of data description was developed in order to simplify the recording of survey data and its standardization. This form includes all general data on the water body, which can be collected without using special devices or equipment.

Introduction

Conducting hydrological studies can be a very complex and difficult task. This manual contains the **simplest procedure for exploring a body of water**, attempting a description, and the preliminary evaluation of its environmental state. This procedure is based on visual examination, requiring no special equipment, instruments or technical devices.

This lesson is designed to be conducted by several groups of students (3-5 pupils), each group studying its own body of water (a small river or a stream). After all the field data has been collected, the groups compare their results. Another option is that one group studies several water bodies and then compares the results.

The following items are **required** for the research: a measuring tape (from 5 to 50 meters long, a pole marked into 10 cm segments, thermometers, plastic bottles for water samples, 10-20 liter plastic bag or bucket, a watch with a second hand and chemical test kits or reagents.

Procedure

General information

The following procedure of exploring the description of a water reservoir can be applied to any small water body: a river, stream, pond, lake or reservoir. Larger bodies such as seas or oceans require other procedures for description.

In order to make recording easier when conducting an exploratory survey, an **Exploratory Description Form** for a water body was developed (Table 1 at the end of this manual). All research is based on filling the form out and analyzing the information.

Filling out the form starts immediately in the field. The data of additional research as well as the results of field data handling will be recorded on the back of the form. Names of those who conducted the survey should also be written on the back of the form.

The following information is to be included on the main (front) part of the form:

1. Date of observation - day, month, year.

2. Weather conditions - weather conditions of the day when the observation was carried out should be described - air temperature in the shade, cloudiness (according to a 10-point scale, where 0 = completely bright sky, and 10 = totally overcast sky), wind strength (no wind, gentle breeze, strong), absence/presence of precipitation, if precipitation is present, then its type (*rain/snow*) and intensity *(slight, strong)*. During cold times of year, occurrence and depth of snow cover on the shore as well as ice and snow on the water surface should be recorded.

3. Type and name of the water body (for example: *Oak Creek, Missouri River,* etc.)

4. Location of the studied area (observation site) - name of the administrative district where the observation site is located and its distance from the nearest human settlement or any other constant landmark (for example, *300 m up/down the town/settlement N, dam, bridge, etc.)*

5. Vicinity description (description of the surrounding environment) - that surrounds the water body. If there is a settlement, then its type (*city, town*), type of housing system (stone many-storied/low-storied buildings, wooden houses, summer houses, sheds (barns), garages, etc.) should be recorded. If there is an industrial zone then its features should be written down, if there is a forest - what kind (*coniferous, deciduous, coniferous-broad leafed*), if there is an agricultural land then it should be specified - *fields, meadows, pastures* etc.

6. Morphometrical features of the site - its width, average dept*h* (in meters), stream velocity (in meters per second), shore type (*sloping, steep, beach, artificial bank*), slope of the bottom (*slopping, abrupt, steep*), if possible, slope in degrees.

All these measurements are taken in the same part of the water body where the survey and observation are carried out.

The width of a waterbed is measured with a tape measure (while

wading, swimming across the river, from a boat or a bridge). Depth is measured with a marked pole in several places depending on the width of the riverbed and bottom structure (it is advisable to take at least 10 measures across the riverbed). Stream velocity is measured along the same section of the river (10-30 meters depending on the size and stream velocity), and measured with a tape measure. Any half-submerged object (an apple, an orange, a closed glass jar etc.) can be used as a float. Measurements of stream velocity are taken several times (not less than three times) and then an average value is estimated.

Estimations of a **cross-section of a waterbed, water output** and **volume of the water flow** are done in the lab based on calculations and measurements of waterbed width, depth and stream velocity.

For those estimations, two values are needed: river cross-section and stream velocity. It is easier to define the river cross-section on a graph by drawing the waterbed profile on graph paper. In a certain scale, the width and depth of the waterbed in different places (the more often measurements are taken, the more accurate the data is) are plotted on the graph. After the riverbed profile is drawn on the plotting paper, the number of full checks "inside" the profile should be counted. Each cell corresponds to a certain square of the river cross-section (the scale is known), and then half-filled cells are counted (their number is totaled and divided by two), then one-third cells (which are totaled and divided by three). All data is added and the number of full cells is counted; this number stands for a stream cross-section value in square meters.

Water output is amount of water that flows through a waterbed per

second. It is estimated by multiplying the waterbed cross-section (in sq. m.) by the average stream velocity (in meters per second).

In the **case of small streams**, and if there is a narrow place (a tube, a waterfall); water output can be measured directly by placing a strong plastic bag or a bucket under the falling flow. Noting the time period (from one to several seconds depending on the stream flow output), one can then measure the volume of the water in the plastic bag (by weighting or pouring into a measuring container) and then estimate the water output without graphical calculations.

Water output is measured in cubic meters per second (or in liters per second for small streams). **Stream flow volume** is estimated by multiplying the value of water output by the desired time (for an hour - by 3,600 seconds, for a 24 hour period - by 86,400 seconds and so on).

A plan of the water body and riverbed cross-section profile can be drawn on the back of the form.

7. Riverside water vegetation – its presence or absence; when present, the **dominant species** should be listed in the order of decreasing abundance.

8. High aquatic vegetation - its presence or absence; when present, the dominant species should be listed in the order of decreasing abundance.

9. Description of the river bottom soil and shore soils

The following information can be used when describing soil type and sedimentation: **stone type** – the bottom is mainly covered with stones; **stone-sand type** – among separate stones there are some places of open soil; **sandy soil** – sand dominates, stones are met rarely; **silt-sandy type** – silt is the dominating part; when the soil is rubbed between fingers, one can feel the presence of sand; **sand-silty type** – the sand is completely or partly covered with silt; **silty** *type* – when the soil is rubbed one cannot feel the presence of sand; *clay type* – when soil is rubbed one can feel clay plasticity; these are typical for artificial water bodies.

The soil is especially important for benthic organisms as well as for high water plants. A soil with a large proportion of silt is typical for water bodies with a high concentration of organic compounds, which cannot be processed by water organisms.

10. General description of water:

a) *Water temperature* – is measured by any thermometer in the shade near a bank and also at some distance from the bank (if it is possible – from a boat, a bridge). The temperature should be read without taking the lower part of the thermometer out of the water. It is advisable to measure water temperature at a depth of 1m (from a boat or a bridge). In order to do this, the thermometer is lowered into the water on a string and after some time it is quickly taken out and the temperature is written down without taking the thermometer completely out of the water.

b) *Water color* – is *absent* (water is transparent) or the color should be specified – *blue, green, yellow-green, green-yellow, yellow, brown-yellow, or brown.* In order to define the color of the water in the water body, the water is poured into a test tube and its color is determined against a white sheet of paper. The test tube can also be compared with a reference standard: distilled water in the same test tube.

The color of water can de defined in two ways - from the side or from above; in both cases it should de determined against a white sheet of paper. If desired, color intensity can be assessed in degrees: 0-10° = no color or it is slightly noticeable, 20-50° = light color, 30-100° = intense color.

c) **Water transparency** can be determined in two ways. When it is possible to determine water transparency directly in the water source (if a boat or a bridge is available), then a **Sekki** disc is used. A Sekki disc is a round white object (a special metal circle or an enameled cover of a saucepan) 30 cm in diameter that is lowered on a string until it is out of sight (it should be dipped from the shadow side of a boat or a bridge). An average of several lifts and sinks is estimated as the water transparence indicator (in meters).

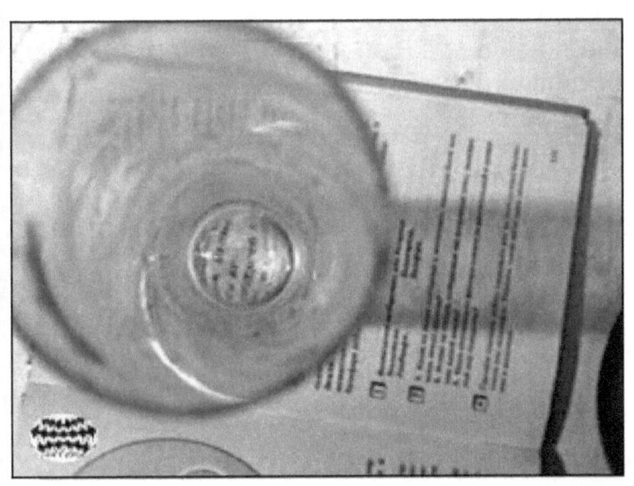

If a high glass cylinder with a clear bottom is available then water transparence can be measured in the following way. The cylinder bottom is placed on clear typed text (with a font of 12 or 13) and then water is poured into the cylinder until the text becomes unreadable. The height of water inside the cylinder is measured (in cm) and it is used as a relative indicator of the water transparence.

d) ***Water smell*** - its presence or absence, if there is smell then it should be identified, for example, *fishy,* ***hydrosulphuric****, grassy, moldy,* ***saprogenic****, marshy, woody, earthy, petrol, aromatic, undefined*. Due to the fact that smell is a personal indicator, it is advised that several people define the smell simultaneously.

It is better to define the smell of water at two different temperatures - 20 and 60 degrees. Heating usually helps to define smell better. In both cases, water is poured into a flask or a jar with a wide neck, and then it is covered with a lid, quickly shaken and then the smell intensity and its nature are determined.

Strength of the smell is assessed according to the following scale:

Grade	Smell	Characteristics
0	No smell	Absence of sensation
1	Very slight	Cannot be defined
2	Slight	Is revealed, but does not attract attention
3	Noticeable	Easily revealed
4	Distinct	The smell is evident; it makes water unusable for drinking
5	Strong	Foul, water is unusable for drinking

11. Characteristics of growth on underwater objects (periphyton).

Growth (**periphyton**) on different underwater objects – *bridge piles, stone and concrete slabs, stems and leaves of high water plants, and other objects* are described.

If periphyton is present then its color, shape and size should be described. The degree of its abundance is estimated visually according to the following scale: very poorly developed – 1 point, slight bloom – 2, moderately developed – 3, abundant – 4, very abundant – 5 points.

The appearance of periphyton is different depending on the water body state. A clear green color (as typical for flowering plants) or brown (like autumn leaves) manifests that algae prevail in periphyton composition: green algae or diatom algae correspondingly. If the green color has a blue tint it means that **cyanobacteria** prevail. White, grey-white, floccose (wooly) growth or flaccid, discolored and slimy prove its extensive bacterial composition and testify to poor environmental conditions of the reservoir.

12. Water surface pollution – presence or absence of extraneous admixtures on the water surface – *oil film, spots, foam, different floating objects, algae gatherings,* etc.

The extent of water surface pollution with oil and oil products as well as their approximate weight can be determined according to the following table:

Grade	General appearance	Characteristics of water surface color	Oil weight on the water surface (g/ sq. m)
0	There are no spots or film on the water surface	Clear water surface without any color at different light conditions	0
1	Separate spots and grey film are visible at a calm state of the water surface	Separate rainbow stripes are visible at the most favorable light conditions and calm water	0.1
		Separate spots and grey film of a silver covering, appearance of clearly visible colors	0.2
2	Visible spots of oil film; not pleasant for swimming	Spots and films with bright rainbow stripes are visible on weak waves	0.4
3	Oil and oil products cover significant areas of the water surface; oil spots cover banks and water vegetation; swimming is impossible	Color transition from rainbow to dim turbid brown	1.2
4	Oil spots and films are met on most parts of the water surface, they are easily seen and not ruptured even at a rough wake; banks and on-shore plants are stained with oil; swimming is impossible	Color is dark; dark-brown	2.4
5	Water surface is completely covered with oil; banks, on-shore plants and facilities are stained with oil; swimming is impossible	Color is black-brown, blue-brown	Over 3

13. Fauna of the water body and its vicinity. The following details should be provided: presence of large (visible with the naked eye) *water **invertebrates**, **insects** flying above the water surface, fish, birds, etc.*

14. Main types of human impact. The following information should be included in the section: presence, intensity and distance from the studied area (for rivers – up the watercourse) of such forms of human activities as: *industrial, household and agricultural sources of pollution (plants, factories, boiler houses, bus stations, dumps, personal garages and summer houses, stockyards* and so on), *bathing* – approximate number of people per a shore distance unit (100 m, 1 km), *cattle watering* – approximate number of heads; *dams; log rafting.*

Main chemical characteristics of water quality

Simple chemical characteristics are measured either directly at the water source or in the laboratory. If water is to be tested in the laboratory then water samples should be collected into ***hermetic*** plastic or glass containers. Sampling rules are simple: 1) water should be poured into the bottle while it is dipped lower than the water surface; 2) before sampling, the bottle should be rinsed several times with water

from the reservoir; 3) the bottle should be filled up to its neck and the lid should be screwed on directly underwater.

A list of water chemical analyses depends on tests and chemical reagents available at school. At the minimum, the following tests should be carried out: **pH** estimation, determination of **nitric** compounds concentration (**ammonium** and **nitrates**), water hardness, as well as dissolved **oxygen** concentration.

Survey data presentation

The results of conducted research should be presented in a text form together with forms of exploratory surveys.

While **preparing the report,** your main attention should be paid to the comparison of several studied bodies of water. In order to compare two or more sites, students should analyze each feature of the water sources, revealing their similarities and differences according to the following plan:

1. Characteristics of water course origin (nature);
2. Characteristics of the valley – age, origin (if possible);
3. Features of the vicinity (vegetation, human activities and so on);
4. Waterway morphology, including water output values;
5. Water and riverside vegetation;
6. Description of the river bottom and banks;
7. Water quality and its chemical features;
8. Peculiarities of the water growth, water surface pollution;
9. Wildlife
10. Brief description of human impact.

Two or more water bodies can be compared; the comparison can be presented in the form of a table.

Table 1.

Exploratory Description Form for a Water Body № ______

1. Date of observation ________________________ (day, month, year)
2. Weather conditions ____
   (air temperature, cloudiness, wind strength, precipitation, snow cover and ice)
3. Type and name of the water body________________________________
4. Location of the studied area (observation site)________________________
____
   (administrative district where the observation site is located and its distance from
   the nearest human settlement)
5. Vicinity description (description of the surrounding environment) ______
____
   (village, town, city, forest, meadows, agricultural lands, etc. and their short
   description)
6. Morphometrical features of the site ________________________________
____
   (width, average depth, stream velocity, shore type, slope of the bottom)
7. Riverside water vegetation (dominant species)________________________
____
8. High aquatic vegetation (dominant species) __________________________
____
9. Description of the river bottom soil and shore soils ___________________
____
   (stone type, stone-sand type, sandy soil, silt-sandy type, sand-silty type, silty type,
   clay type)
10. General description of water:
a) water temperature: near a bank _________ , far from a bank __________ ,
at a depth of 1 m ________ b) water color ________________________
        (blue, green, yellow-green, green-yellow, yellow, brown-yellow, or brown)
c) water transparency ____
                (technique of measurement – Sekki disc/glass cylinder)
d) water smell
____
        (its presence or absence, description and strength)
11. Characteristics of growth on underwater objects (periphyton) ________
____
        (color, shape and size)

12. Water surface pollution _______________________________________

____

(oil film, spots, foam, different floating objects, algae gatherings, etc. and their extend)

13. Fauna of the water body and its vicinity _______________________________

____

(water invertebrates, insects flying above the water surface, fish, birds, etc.)

14. Main types of human impact _______________________________

____

____

(industrial, household and agricultural sources of pollution: presence, intensity and distance from the studied area)

Authors of the description _______________________________

Study of Snow Cover Profile

This manual describes the main functions and features of snow cover, and a procedure for snow survey along a landscape profile. The activity includes location of survey sites, establishment of snow exploring shaft, determination of snow layers according to a number of visual characteristics, their measurement and description.

Introduction

One of the most important landscape characteristics in winter are the **properties of snow cover** – its thickness and density, as well as depth of the frost zone at different sites. It is well known that preservation of seeds and sprouts from winterkill as well as the wintering success of many animal species depends on the depth of the soil frost zone.

Depth of the seasonal frost zone is of great importance, as it influences peculiarities of spring soil erosion causing destruction of soil structure. Unfortunately, the study of permafrost is complicated by its laboriousness and use of specific equipment, for example, the soil probe. Thus, this educational activity will be focused on snow – i.e. peculiarities of its distribution along the relief forms and under different vegetation types, structure of snow cover and study of snow's role in landscape function.

The activity is aimed at revealing the **dependence** of the thickness and structure of snow cover upon **relief forms** and **vegetation type**. It is known that snow cover is thinner and distributed unevenly in coniferous forests.

In contrast, the distribution of snow in deciduous forests is thicker and more evenly distributed. In comparing a forest and an open site, it turns out that wind is much lighter in forests than in open areas, so snow is not blown off the soil surface. Thus, snow cover in forests is characterized by a more even distribution than in the field, for instance, where wind differentiates thickness of the snow cover by stripping rises and filling up relief depressions with snow.

In order to complete the task, students will require shovels (for unearthing snow), rulers (it is recommended to use long rulers – for the full depth of the snow cover) or measuring tapes, description forms (soil description forms can be used) or field logs, compasses and some other materials at hand (sticks, blades and matches).

The teacher should explain the main functions and properties of the snow cover before the activities, and students should be taught how to measure and describe the snow cover prior to independent studies.

Main functions of snow cover

The role of snow in the function of an environment is especially obvious when air temperature falls below zero degrees centigrade. In areas where there is no snow in cold seasons, soil gets frozen through for many meters, and, for instance, in Yakutia, the depth of permafrost makes up one and a half kilometer.

The preservative function of snow or **thermal insulation** is, perhaps, the most important one. It is known that snow cover has loose structure due to the different shapes of snowflakes. Interstices

among snowflakes are filled up with air that is characterized by *low heat conductivity*, so we owe such a wonderful property of snow to air. The air, as we sometimes (but incorrectly) say, "warms up well."

Due to the low heat conductivity of snow, day-to-day temperature variation penetrates into the snow cover only for a depth of 24 centimeters on average. As specific research has shown, if the amplitude of temperature fluctuation reaches 30 degrees at the snow surface, then at 5 cm depth it amounts to only 16 degrees, at 24 cm depth it makes up 3 degrees and at 44 cm depth the amplitude is insignificant – 0.8 degrees.

Not just soils are protected from frost penetration due to snow as mentioned above, but plants as well, which can stay green through the winter. They often serve as the only food for animals, and harbor seeds, which serve as security for renewal of the vegetation cover in spring.

However, snow is known not only for its heat insulating function. As snow is water in solid aggregative state, it **accumulates** in large quantities and remains until spring in order to water the earth and allow plants to start growing when it becomes warm.

Besides heat insulating and accumulating functions, snow cover also exerts **influence upon a climate.**

Everyone knows that air masses move around the earth's surface. Coming from remote areas, they bring along characteristics of the area they originated from – mainly air **humidity** and **temperature**. As they move above the surface continuously, they change slightly; however, if they stagnate in one area for a certain time, they acquire temperature and moisture characteristics of the given region.

It is also known that air cannot be heated directly by the sun. Sunlight is absorbed by a surface and then the surface gives heat back to the air in the form of infrared radiation. Some solar radiation is reflected by the surface in the form of light and is not transformed into heat. The less is the surface reflection power and the higher its absorption capacity, the warmer the surface becomes. Thus, surface temperature depends on its reflection properties, or *albedo*.

The albedo of a black body is equal to 0%, whereas the albedo of a white body is equal to 100%. Fresh-fallen snow is very close to 100% according to its albedo. Correspondingly, when the ground is covered with snow, the ground cannot warm up air anymore. So, air is cooled. Hence, winter temperature conditions are partly kept by this phenomenon. So if, at last, the sun peeps out and one would think it can become warmer, it does not happen. Spring and the corresponding rise in temperature are brought by warm air masses that have been warmed up in other regions of the Earth, which are not covered with snow.

One more significant characteristic of snow is that snow **clears the atmosphere** from mechanical and chemical pollution. Smog over a city, which consists of acid deposition, exhaust gases, aerosols and radionuclids in different forms, disappears after a snowfall. However, this fact does not make plants happy, as melting snow gives all absorbed pollutants back to the soil in spring.

Main properties of snow cover

Structure of snow cover is characterized by such significant properties (values) as **thickness** and **density**, which are closely interrelated. They depend on a number of factors, including amount of precipitation, temperature conditions, peculiarities of relief and vegetation.

Thickness of the snow cover grows in the course of winter and it reaches its maximum value in March (in regions in Central Russia). The snow depth could be maximum too, if it did not compact under the influence of thaws, its own gravity force and other reasons.

Snow is greatly intertwined and compacted under the influence of a wind at open sites, thus there is little snow left in some places and high snowdrifts are formed in others. The wind loses its power within forests and it barely shifts snow masses. However, even within the forest, snow cover is uneven, but due to other reasons. Most snow is accumulated at forest glades and in open spaces among trees, in desolated roads and paths. The shallowest depth of snow is found around tree trunks as thick snowflakes remain on tree branches and form a "snow overhang" or "*kukhta*", which becomes bigger from one

snowfall till another, especially when it is calm. Kukhta can become very large in some geographical regions. Coniferous trees in forests in the middle Urals get covered with such a strong shell made of frozen snow that it is difficult to break it with a stick. Thick kukhta covers lower branches of spruce up to three and more meters high completely in March.

Due to formation of even thinner kukhta than in the Urals there is less snow under the forest canopy and it is distributed unevenly. More snow is found in deciduous forests, considerably less snow is characteristic of pine forests and especially little snow is registered in spruce, fir and cedar dark-coniferous forests.

Initial density of the snow cover depends on weather conditions when the snow falls and, consequently, on the form of falling snowflakes. Snowflakes represent compound multifaceted stars in calm weather and light frost. Such snowflakes easily grapple with each other, forming loose flakes, which fall down slowly and quietly and create a fluffy shroud. Much air remains among the facets of snowflakes and because of this, snow obtains its blinding whiteness that is characteristic of fresh-fallen snow. However, snowflakes lose their facets in the course of time due to the effects of their own gravity force as well as other reasons. They turn into simple ice crystals that fit closer and closer together so that the snow gradually gets compacted.

Snow density and, primarily, density of the top snow layer is intensively influenced by a strong wind. It is clear that **wind's greatest influence** is exerted in open spaces – in fields, vast swamps and large water bodies. There, compact crust is quite often

formed on the surface of snow cover; it is also called "a wind board."

The role of wind is considerably smaller in forests, not taking into account certain sites that border windward forest edges. Snow is compacted under the influence of its own weight in temperature differences in forests, whereas under tree crowns it is rammed by the heavy weight of falling kukhta.

Snow density becomes greater under the influence of all the above-mentioned factors; the snow is more intensively compacted at the end of winter and in early spring.

Snow gradually loses its initial whiteness in the course of time; moreover, it gets littered even in dense forests far from any human settlements and busy roads with their smoke and ash. It gets littered with old needles, small twigs, seeds and other natural forest debris.

When snow falls in hard frost and with a strong wind, then we observe not the above-mentioned compound stars but ice crystals and even needles which prick our faces so painfully in snowstorms. Such snowflakes fall down, fit together tightly and immediately form a compact snow cover.

Ice crusts that differ in thickness, compactness and located at different depths are formed as a result of temperature drops, which are quite often registered before winter and in the course of winter months when thaws are replaced by frost. Some ice crusts appear on the threshold of winter close to the ground surface or surround and "lock" the ground herbage. They are called "ground-glass" and cause many difficulties to wintering animals as they prevent animals from getting food, digging snow, and moving freely in snow.

Ice crusts are quite often formed on the snow surface itself, in the form of a thin crust of ice over snow. If this thin crust is then covered with a layer of fresh-fallen snow and it is repeated several times during winter, then buried ice crusts appear within the snow cover.

Besides formation of different ice crusts, the structure of snow, especially its lower layers, undergoes great changes and obtains a *macrocrystalline structure* in the course of time.

Snow Survey at the Profile

Organization of field activities

Optimal organization of training activities within the framework of the given educational task is to have students work at the same site where a slope profile has been established (see "Plotting a Profile of a River Valley Slope" manual, above) and soil and geobotanical studies have taken place (see "Integrated Study Based on Landscape Profile", below).

In any case, it is recommended to study snow cover at a section of the river (stream) valley slope where **different relief types** are represented, including depressions around the river-bed, floodplain, terraces (flat areas in the lower course of macrorelief), watershed (a flat area located at a certain eminence), slopes of different steepness, as well as **different plant associations** including a meadow association, a deciduous forest, a mixed forest, a pine and a spruce forest (ideally).

It is convenient when a length of the profile is not large – from 200 m up to 1 km. It will be easier to organize activities of different teams at such a section.

A group of students consisting of 10-15 people is divided into teams of two. Each team is given a task to describe a number of certain points along the profile. Selection of points (description sites) is determined by a number of student teams and the diversity of conditions along the profile line. Description should cover all the present diversity of relief forms and vegetation types; in addition, it is advised to make descriptions under different conditions – for instance, under the tree crown and at a certain distance away from the tree, for instance, in the clearing. However, it is not necessary to carry out the descriptions in such pairs everywhere – it is enough to make two such descriptions in each forest type (under a birch and in the clearing within the birch forest, under a pine and in the clearing in stand of pine trees, under a spruce and in the clearing within the spruce forest, etc.)

Description of snow cover

A **Snow pit** is established at a site in order to describe the snow cover. This is a pit in the snow, of a size large enough so that it is possible to get into the snow pit without destroying of the snow pit wall (usually 1.5 m x 1.5 m). The snow pit is dug with a shovel for the whole depth of the snow cover – to the ground below. Unlike a soil pit, the wall of the snow pit should not be located facing the sun. Even in frosty weather, the sun can quickly warm up snow and it will change the picture for the description of snow features.

The snow from the pit should also be put at one of the sides as when digging a soil pit, the front wall (the wall prepared for description) should not be touched or stepped on and snow should not be put close to it.

When the snow pit is dug out, first topsoil vegetation should be described (before it is trampled down) – approximate plant composition is taken down (if there are green plants, they should be described separately) and their approximate numbers (projective percent of cover). Ground properties are determined together with a description of topsoil vegetation – whether it is frozen or not, then its **temperature** should be taken. If there is no soil thermometer, it can be done with a regular one. A small cavity in the ground is made with the help of a pen or a stick and the head of a regular thermometer is placed into the cavity for one minute. It is recommended to write down the temperature without taking the thermometer out of the ground. Choose a site for measuring ground temperature not in the middle of the study area (as ground changes its temperature very quickly there) but under the snow pit wall itself.

Measure the temperature **inside** the snow cover immediately before the description –place a thermometer into two or three loose layers at different depths for one minute. This data, together with temperature of the ground under the scow cover and air temperature (it can be measured at a person's height) will provide additional interesting information on heat-conducting properties of snow.

The next stage of field studies is **snow cover description** itself. The vertical front snow wall should be **smoothed out** – a thin layer of snow should be peeled off the whole depth of the shaft with a shovel edge – top-down so that the snow will be fresh and clean, immediately before the description. The front wall should be as even and vertical as possible.

The first stage of description is measurement of the **total thickness** of the snow cover. Snow cover depth is measured with a ruler (it is recommended to have long rulers, which will be long enough to measure the whole thickness of the snow) or a measuring tape.

Then students proceed with the most difficult stage of the description – determination of borders of snow horizons (layers). For this purpose, the front wall is closely examined and probed according to the following characteristics of each layer: color, graininess, moisture and density (hardness).

The **color** is determined visually according to the following four classes (in compliance with a standard): *white, white-gray, gray and bluish gray*.

Three gradations are defined according to structure of the snow (**graininess**): *fine-grain, medium-grained* and *coarse-grained* snow.

Two gradations are determined in accordance with **moisture**: a *dry* snow – which forms fragile snowballs, pours off the shovel and is usually loose and friable; and *wet* – which forms sticky, firm snowballs that are easily made, and can form snow blocks.

Four gradations of snow are defined according to **density** (solidity): *fresh-fallen* (very soft), *packed* (soft), *compacted* (hard) and *solid* (very hard). Snow density can be measured the following way: four fingers easily penetrate into very soft snow, only one finger can penetrate into soft snow, whereas hard snow can be permeated only by a pencil, and very hard snow – only by a knife. Granulated snow (firn) and ice are described separately when determining density of snow cover. Firn is an intermediate state between snow and ice – it consists of compacted grains of ice, but it is not yet ice.

Layers of snow cover are first determined visually (defining their color and graininess) and by moving a fingertip gently along the snow wall (upwards) trying to feel changes in density and structure of snow layers. Change in any of above-described properties of snow is an indicator of a layer border. To make the following measurements easier it is possible to mark borders between snow layers by putting objects into the snow – twigs, blades of grass, matches.

When determining the density of snow, i.e. moving a fingertip along

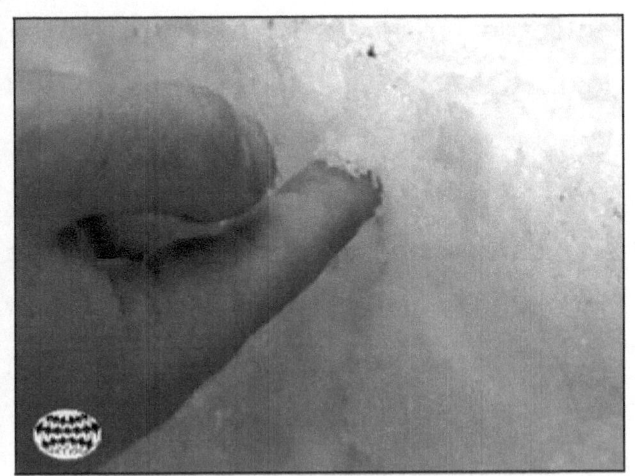

the wall, it is necessary to note presence of thin crusts of ice (on the snow surface), ice streaks within the snow cover – buried crusts as well as the presence of ice on the surface of ground or herbage (ground crust). Such crusts are also recorded, even though they can be very thin (sometimes they are less than 1 mm thick).

The next stage is measuring the thickness of each layer and their description.

To make the description easier it is possible to use **forms** that are similar to forms of soil profile description (or use those forms instead, see "Simple Procedure of Soil Description" manual, above). It is also possible not to go beyond drawing of schemes in the field diary.

In any case it is suggested to **plot borders between snow layers** on the scheme (which are measured with the help of a ruler) upwards – where ground surface is taken for zero (start). The thickness of each layer (it is measured directly or calculated later according to a scheme) and its properties should be drawn and described on the scheme of snow cover structure. Similar to a description of soil horizons, verbal descriptions of each snow layer should be given by hand on the right of the drawing, opposite the given layer on the scheme.

The concluding stage of field description is **associated data**. Similar to soil description, associated data includes the date, time and authors of the description, geographical and local situation (region, area, human settlement and so on), position of the snow shaft (its location in relief, within the landscape profile; it is recommended to write down direction of the slope relative to North and South if possible), description of surrounding tree-and-shrubby vegetation (name of the plant association, formula of the forest stand, density of crowns and height of trees) as well as peculiarities of the given snow shaft (under a tree, at a glade, with its distance to the closest tree, etc.) The more small details of the snow shaft location recorded the better.

Lab studies of materials

When students come back to the laboratory, they should collect and arrange all descriptions made during field studies. This should result in a drawing of the landscape profile (a relief line) with shown conventions of the snow cover properties.

The first stage is **unification** of the description. It consists of the detection of certain common properties of all described snow pits – for instance, presence of the same number of main layers (usually there are only three to five layers which are parted by ice crusts). At this stage the teacher should analyze independent studies of students and check that there are not too many layers found (sometimes it is possible to count more layers than there are, due to excessive eagerness of some students) or – on the contrary – too little. It is suggested that the teacher should check several description sites in order to make description results reliable.

Then a system of **conventions** should be developed. They are mainly applied to a pictorial rendition of graininess and density of snow layers. Snow density is usually expressed with the help of color: the denser the layer, the darker the color.

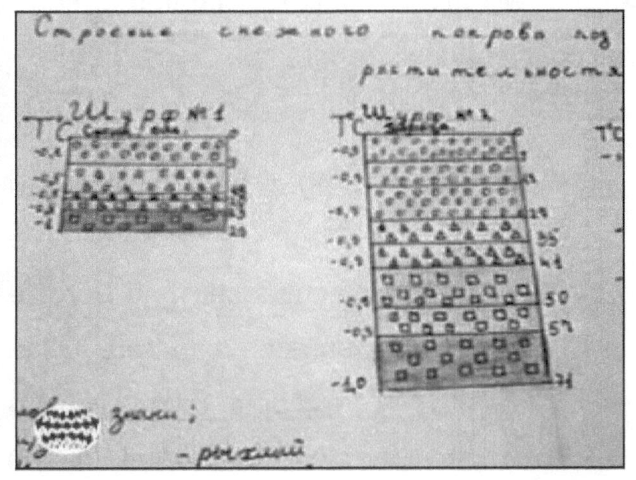

Different tints of the color are used: from light blue in case of fresh-fallen, very soft snow to dark blue in case of firm snow and black – for ice crusts. Graininess is shown with the help of symbols, for instance, in dots or circles of different size.

A **snow column**, i.e. a scheme of snow profile section according to a chosen scale (vertical scale which reflects thickness of snow cover) is drawn for each described snow pit along the profile line. When drawing a profile it is recommended to select a uniform scale for all the snow shafts, whereas the columns are plotted below the relief line in the sites on the profile where descriptions have been carried out.

In order to make the snow cover scheme more pictorial, it can be expressed not only with the help of columns along the profile line but also with a firm line above the relief line (vertical scale which reflects the total thickness of snow cover and is chosen arbitrarily). It can be done if descriptions have been carried out more or less evenly along the whole length of the profile (of course, extrapolating to sections between description sites). Such line will vividly show the total thickness of the snow cover along the profile line and, if vegetation is plotted on the profile drawing, it will allow to link regularities of snow cover distribution with previously studied landscape components – relief and vegetation.

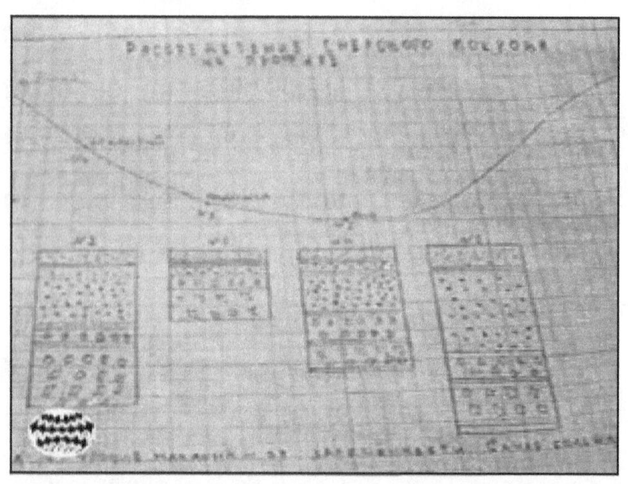

Thus, the activity can result in drawing of a landscape profile scheme, where the following information is plotted: 1) relief line, 2) tree-and-shrubby vegetation; 3) line of the total thickness of the snow cover (along the whole length of the profile) and 4) columns/schemes of snow pit sections at different sites along the profile with detailed pictures of properties of different snow layers.

The following **questions** should be discussed in order to determine comprehension of fulfilled studies:

1. What is the general connection between the snow cover, relief and vegetation?

2. Besides total precipitation, what factors influence formation of the snow cover?

3. What role does the snow cover play in the lives of plants and animals (temperature, water reserve)?

4. It is necessary to reconstruct the course of weather conditions in the given winter (a number of thaws and snowfalls) and to answer the question: "How did vegetation and relief adjust weather peculiarities last winter in ways that are common for the given area?"

Physical and Chemical Properties of Natural Waters

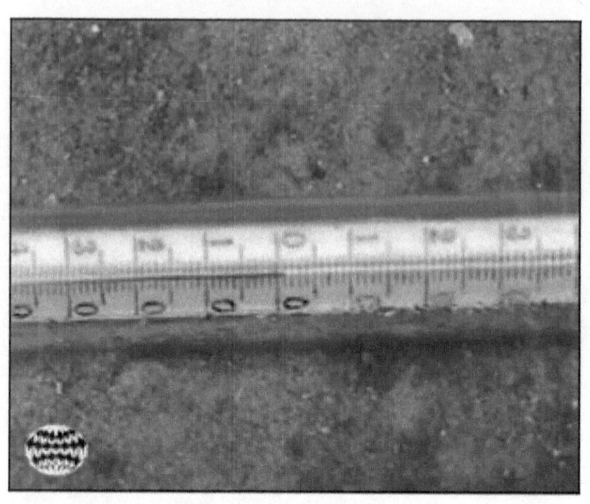

This manual contains guidelines for sampling natural and artificial bodies of water and snow sampling. It describes the procedure for determining the main physical properties of water including temperature, transparency, coloration, smell and total content of dredge and suspended particles. Quantitative analyses include acid estimation and oxygen content.

Introduction

Natural water contains many components that are found in low (less than 1%) and ultra-low (less than 1 one part per million) concentrations. In Russia, the state system of monitoring carries out the monitoring of natural and drinking water quality according to more than 50 parameters. In order to insure that water quality complies with special requirements, monitoring is carried out according to 100 or more components; many of them amount to one billionth and trillionth of a toxic substance (micrograms and nanograms of the substance per 1 liter of water). Certainly, such analyses are based on the application of modern and expensive equipment as well as the high qualifications of an analyst.

This manual focuses on only the **simplest parameters**; their determination will allow students to make a preliminary conclusion on water quality and characterize the purity of the water body.

This educational activity is aimed at water sampling from as **many water sources as possible** found within the vicinity of the school or field center as well as at comparison of some of the simplest physical and chemical properties of water taken from those sources.

Empty plastic bottles with screw-caps (one bottle per each water source), a shovel or a scoop, a glass cylinder about 50 cm high, different test-kits for determining water properties and clean plastic bags are required for this assignment.

Sampling

Sampling sites

When carrying out the given work, students should try to take water from a maximum number of sources in the area – both from natural water bodies and artificial ones. Water can be taken from local streams, rivers, lakes, ponds and water reservoirs (depending on their availability in the area) as well as from wells, water pipes, rainwater barrels, garden pools, etc. Snow samples should also be taken.

General rules of water sampling

Water sampling is an important part of water analysis and a necessary requirement for the reliability of obtained results and their applicability in practice. Mistakes arising from improper water sampling cannot be corrected later.

There are a number of general rules of water sampling for further analyses regardless of the source of water samples.

1) **A standard type of container** should be used as jars for all water sampling. At present it is more convenient to use clear 1-2-litre bottled water plastic bottles for these purposes. They should be washed beforehand without use of detergents and then dried out.

2) Prior to water sampling, the bottle should be **rinsed several times** with the water under study.

3) The bottle should be **filled with water up to the very top** and the cap should be screwed so that there is absolutely no air left in the bottle.

4) In all water sources, the bottle should be **immersed into water completely** (with the exception of a faucet). It should be placed 10 cm lower the water surface so that water surface film does not go into the bottle.

5) When sampling water, it is necessary to **measure water temperature** regardless of the water source. Temperature can be taken with the help of a regular thermometer, which should be immersed into water for a minute. The temperature should be read

without taking the thermometer out of the water. When sampling water running from the faucet, the head of a thermometer is placed into the water current right at the faucet outlet.

6) Each bottle containing a water sample should be **labeled immediately** at the sampling site. Students must also record details of the water sampling in their field notebooks. It is sufficient to write down the name of the water source and the number of the sample on the bottle in indelible marker. It is advised to write prior to sampling, when the bottle is dry. More detailed information is taken down in the field notebook. It usually includes the following standard data: the number of the water sample, the date, time and authors of the sample, geographical and local position of the sampling site (region, district, human settlement, name of the water body, position of the site in relation to other landmarks and so on (more details – the better). The method of water sampling should also be described (from a bank, from a boat, from a bridge, out of a well-bucket, from under a faucet, etc.), as well as water temperature at the moment of sampling.

7) After a sample has been taken, it is necessary to observe the **basic rules of sample storage**: it is advised to carry out the main analyses in the course of an hour from the moment of sampling (especially analyses of smell, transparency and oxygen content (if needed). Other parameters can be determined in the days after samples have been taken. If determination of water properties cannot be conducted at once, the sample should be preserved (each component or a group of substances is characterized with an

independent procedure for preservation) or stored in the refrigerator at a temperature of 3-4 degrees Celsius no longer than 3-5 days.

Techniques of water-sampling

Two techniques of water sampling are applied in environmental monitoring: one-time and multiple. In case of a **one-time sampling**, the water sample is taken once in a certain place. However, one-time water sampling is not enough for valid conclusions on the state of the water body, as in most cases water quality varies in different locations within the same water-body and in different seasons. Nevertheless, conditions of the given educational activity do not allow to take samples many times, i.e. do not involve serial sampling. However, information how it can be done can be useful for students, thus, it is given in a footnote.

When conducting **multiple sampling**, each sample is taken in specific relation to all the other ones. **Zonal sampling** can serve as a typical example. While carrying out **zonal sampling**, samples are taken at different depths along a chosen range (line) of a water reservoir, a lake or a river. A series of samples are usually taken for determination of seasonal or diurnal changes in water properties. Sampling should be carried out taking into account hydrological season (flood or low-water period) when defining seasonal changes.

So-called **matched samples** represent a specific type of serial (multiple) sampling. The samples are taken in different locations along the river's stream current taking into account water flow-through time. A fishing float can be used as a control, it is sent downstream in o90 rder to control water flow from one point to another. Source of pollution or a wastewater discharge points can easily be found out in the course of such sampling.

Averaged sample of flowing water is taken at places with the strongest current.

Sampling in water-bodies

A site for water sampling at the water body is chosen according to a preliminary study of the area. All conditions (season, precipitation,

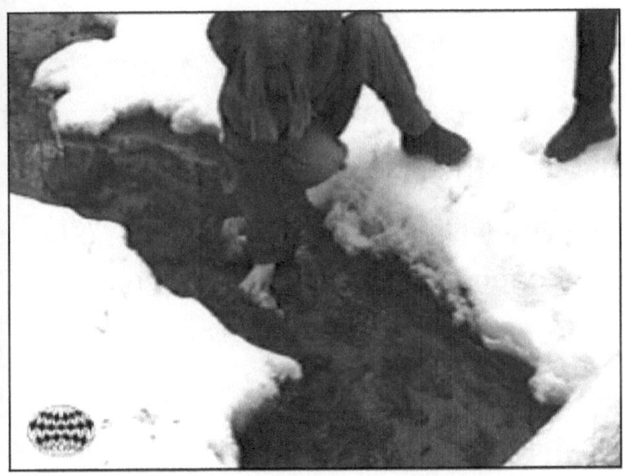

location of potential and known sources of pollution, etc.) that can influence the composition of the sample should be taken into consideration. It is necessary to pay special attention to the **presence of tributaries and sources of river basin pollution**, which may be located upstream of the sampling site. All of the aforementioned conditions can influence the results of analyses and will help then to explain revealed differences among water sources.

Students should be governed by the following **rules when selecting a specific site** for water sampling at water bodies:

1) Water sampling should be conducted at typical, meaning average in all respects, water body segments – at a section of open water, if possible, with an average current and at sites of average depth.

2)   It is advised to **avoid taking samples of stagnant water** in front of dams, in river bends, in dead river branches, etc. In particular, obvious, polluted, stagnant places should be avoided.

Snow sampling

Snow sampling is not a primary activity of this lesson, it is used only for the comparison of the physical and chemical composition of melting water with other water sources in the vicinity of the school or field study center. However, analysis of snow properties can be quite interesting in itself, as it can provide much toward an understanding of air pollution conditions in the given area.

Snow, which have fallen in winter, accumulates many pollutants which precipitate from air and are contained in snow itself. Snow represents peculiar chemical chronicles of the winter. Snow cover pollution can be determined independently with the help of the procedure for complete snow survey or snow survey along a landscape profile (see "Study of Snow Cover Profile" manual) with subsequent analysis of taken samples according to main parameters. At the same time students can make a **map** of snow cover pollution and find out main air pollution **sources**, as well as to determine degree and frontiers of their impact. It is easier to reveal such sources of pollutants as boilers, motor transport, plants and factories belonging to heavy and energy industries.

There are peculiarities in the procedure for snow sampling for the purposes of physical and chemical analyses. Three snow samples should be taken at the same place in order to obtain valid data. It is done as follows:

1)   A **site for snow sampling** is chosen so that it is possible to plot a triangle on it, and its sides should be not less than 10 m long (10-30 m).

2)   **Squares one meter to a side** should be marked off at vertices of the plotted triangle, so we end up with three such squares.

3)   The snow is taken with the help of **"an envelope" technique** in these squares, i.e. samples are taken in the corners of the square (four samples) and in the center of the square. All together, five samples are taken from each square, and all the samples are combined and used for one analysis. So three squares in the vertices of a triangle make up 15 samples, i.e. in five samples for each separate analysis.

4)   Snow is taken from almost the **whole depth of the snow cover**. This is done in order to summarize all the pollution accumulated in the snow during winter. The snow is sampled either with a cylinder, a shovel or a scoop.

All fifteen samples are put into a clean plastic bag. Students should bear in mind that snow volume should be rather big; taking into account the fact that when snow melts its volume will reduce approximately 10 times. So if you have to obtain, for instance, 1 liter of melt water, you have to collect about 10 liters of snow (about a bucket).

Snow can be taken barehanded (make sure that your hands are clean), but students should avoid touching the inner surface of the plastic bag. The plastic bag with snow is tied and packed into the second bag. A piece of paper with sample description and its marking label should be put into the second plastic bag. Plastic bags can be stored in the refrigerator or on the porch.

Prior to analyses, the snow from the plastic bag should be melted and warmed to room temperature. If the bag is waterproof, it is enough just to put the bag in a warm room and leave it there for 2-3 hours, or to take the snow out into a clean enamel basin or into a bucket.

Determination of general physical and chemical properties of water

The main physical parameters measured are temperature, smell, transparency (optical transmission) and coloration. Determination of the content of suspended particles and solutes require some simple equipment.

The **main chemical parameters** that can be measured depend on availability of equipment, reagents or test-kits for analyses of water properties at the school or field study center.

At minimum, an optimal case includes analyses of the following water properties: acidity (pH), total or carbonate water hardness, contents of nitrates or ammonium. It is more interesting (and more expensive) to obtain data on the content of dissolved oxygen, carbon dioxide, iron and phenols. Nevertheless, most analyses can be made with the use of test-kits that are in stores. Let us focus on the procedures of the simplest analyses.

Temperature

As mentioned above, temperature measurement at water sampling is an integral part of the analysis. Temperature should be taken again prior to the main analyses in the laboratory. Large differences in temperature can have an influence upon some results, for instance, pH.

Transparency (optical transmission)

Water transparency depends on **water coloration and turbidity**. Water transparency can be measured at the sampling site with the help of a so-called Sekki disc. It is a white disk 30 cm in diameter (for instance, the white cover of an enamel bucket), which is sunk on a rope into the water from a boat or a bridge. The depth where the disk disappears is measured and taken for a relative value of water transparency. However, although this technique it is a professional method, is labor-intensive and not always available, so we recommend another technique for the given educational purposes – with the help of printing type.

A glass cylinder measuring 40-60 cm tall (usually available with chemical laboratory glassware) is used for determining water transparency. It is placed on a qualitative printing type of a standard size - 3.5 mm (for instance on a book page) in the laboratory at normal room lighting. Then the water under study is slowly poured into the cylinder while a student looks at the printing type from above, through the column of poured water. Water is added to the cylinder until the letters become blurred and the text is not readable. This height is taken for water transparency. Again as in the case with measurement of water transparency using the *Sekki disc*, the obtained value is a relative parameter, meaning that the results can be compared with other results only if they have been obtained with

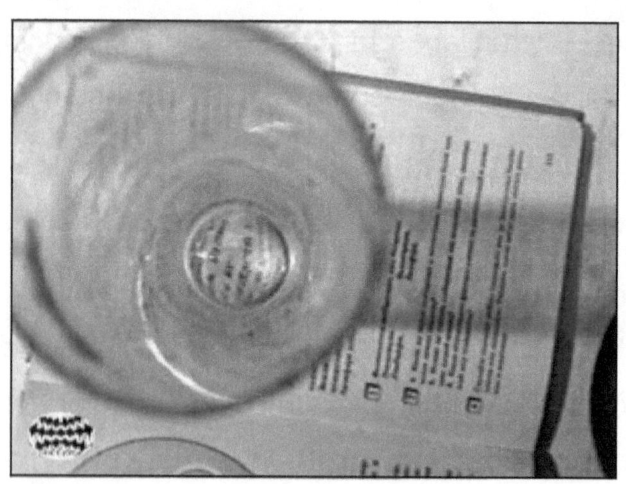

the help of the same procedure.

Both above-described procedures for determination of water transparency are widely accepted as standard. In the first case, water transparency is measured in meters, in the second case – in centimeters.

Data on water transparency indicate not only the degree of saturation of water with suspended particles, but the depth of sunlight penetration into the body of water as well.

Coloration

Water color is determined simultaneously as the measurement of water transparency.

Professional hydrologists and hydrochemists determine water color in field conditions with the help of a color scale consisting of 22 glass test-tubes filled with color solutions of different tints from blue to brown. In order to determine water color with the help of the mentioned technique, a Sekki disc is immersed into water at the depth equal to half of the transparency value. Then the water color against the white disc is compared to the color of the solutions in test-tubes. A color is determined and marked with the number of the corresponding test-tube.

A simple technique, but not as precise as the previous one, is  suggested for the purposes of this educational activity, using the same glass cylinder, which has been used for measurement of water transparency. Before the water is poured out of the cylinder, it is placed on a piece of white paper and the **color of the water inside the cylinder is defined visually**. Water color is described according to the following standard scale: colorless, blue, green, yellow-green, green-yellow, yellow, brownish yellow, light brown, fulvous (dull brown/tawny). Turbid water should be drained prior to determination of its color. Ideally if there is another glass cylinder available, it can be filled with distilled water or pure absolutely colorless water for comparison.

Smell

Water smell is caused by **volatile odorous substances**, which come into water naturally or with wastewater. Wastewater pollution is revealed not only according to their smell, but also according to the smell of the products of their decomposing components.

Some types of aquatic organisms have specific smells, which resemble, for instance, smell of *cucumber (Synura)*, *violets (Mallomonas), pigsty (Anabaena)* and so on.

The smell of wastewater coming from human settlements is a mixture of feces odor with smells of soap, grease, and putrefaction (hydrogen sulfide), and is quite distinctive. Wastewater coming from coal thermal treatment is characterized with a smell of phenols (distinct heavy pharmaceutical smell), resins, hydrogen sulfide, etc.

Water smell is determined at **20 and 60 degrees Celsius**. The smell is described verbally, for instance, "earthy", "fecal", "putrid", "grassy", "moldy", "musty." The smell of chemical substances might be described as "phenol", "resinous", " organic solvent", "iodine", etc. Determination of smell intensity and nature depends on experience and the individual abilities of the researcher, so it is advised to determine the nature of the smell collectively in order to avoid subjective estimations.

The **technical procedure for smell determination** is as follows: 250 ml of water is poured into a flask at 20 degrees Celsius. The flask is capped and its contents are thoroughly shaken several times. Then the flask is opened and smell should be determined immediately. Another flask is warmed in a water bath (or in a drying oven) up to 60 degrees Celsius. The neck of the flask should be covered with a watch crystal. Flask contents are stirred and the smell and its intensity are determined immediately.

Smell intensity is determined by dilution of the sample with distilled water until smell disappears.

Total content of suspended particles and solutes

All substances found in water can be divided into **suspended particles** and **solutes**. In practice, determination of suspended particles consists of water filtration, subsequent drying of a filter and its accurate weighing. The procedure for determination of solute content consists in evaporation of strained water and the subsequent weighing of evaporated residuum.

This task should be performed in the course of this activity only in case if an analytical balance, a drying oven and filters for quantitative determination are available at the school or field study center.

Prior to work, one or two paper filters out of a bundle of filters are checked. Each dried and weighted filter is rinsed with 100 ml of distilled water and then it is dried and weighted again. The loss in weight should be not more than 10% of the filter's weight.

Each filter should be dried and weighed before use. Then a volume of mixed sample (100 – 500 ml depending on the purity of water) is measured off and filtered through a funnel. The filter with filter cake is dried first in air and then in a drying oven to its constant weight at a temperature equal to 105 degrees Celsius. Then the filter is weighed. The amount of suspended particles in the sample is calculated according to the weight difference of a dried filter before and after use. Then the content of suspended substances is estimated per a unit of water volume (g/l).

Determination of snow contamination according to the amount of dust particles (suspended particles) is of particular interest when precision analytical balance is not available. This procedure is considerably simpler than the study of natural water with low concentration of dredge, though it is similar to the above-described process. Melt water, which is obtained from snow samples, is thoroughly mixed and poured through a weighed dry paper filter (it is advised to filter not less than 1 liter of water through it). A filter with filter cake consisting of suspended particles is dried in a drying oven and then weighed. Studies of snow can result in making a map of snow cover pollution in the vicinity of the school, and if taking into account a wind rose, it is possible to discover the main plants that pollute the environment and to prove transport contribution to environmental pollution.

Solutes are determined by evaporation of an already strained water sample. First it is necessary to weigh a porcelain cup, then an appropriate amount of filtered water is poured into the cup and its contents are evaporated in a drying oven.

If total mineralization exceeds 5 g/l, then solute can be detected with the help of procedures of qualitative analysis. If mineralization is less than 5 g/l it is useless to make a qualitative analysis in school laboratory conditions.

Some qualitative chemical analyses

Qualitative determination (i.e. determination of the presence or absence of a substance in the sample) of some of the most widespread solute admixtures is carried out with the help of following reaction.

Determination of nitrates

Nitrates are found almost in all types of waters. A large content of nitrates indicates past pollution with sewage (fecal) waters. The determination of nitrates in underground waters serves as an evaluation of mineralization when water is drained through soil layers. When studying surface waters, the presence of nitrates can serve as an indicator of **waste nitrification**. Violations of mineral fertilizer application procedures can serve as a source of nitrates in areas of intensive agricultural development.

The following analyses are made in order to determine the presence of nitrates in water. Two ml of a test sample is dropped into 5 ml of concentrated sulfuric acid in a test-tube that is constantly stirred. Then a very small amount of solid brucine (careful, it is a powerful poison!) is added and the mixture is stirred again. A resulting yellow or mahogany coloration indicates the presence of nitrates. Sensitivity of the reaction is 1 mg/l and higher.

Determination of sulfates

The presence of sulfates – salts of sulfuric acid - can be increased in water bodies due to **discharge of wastewater** containing inorganic and organic sulfur compounds.

The following procedure is used for determining the presence of sulfates. Approximately 10 ml of the water sample is acidified in a test-tube with several drops of hydrochloric acid and then about 0.5 ml of 10% solution of barium chloride ($BaCl_2$) or barium nitrate ($BaNO_3$) is added to the mixture.

If sulfate content is about 5-50 mg/l, then a slight turbidity appears. If the concentration of sulfates is higher, then precipitate of barium sulfate (nitrate) BaSO4 falls out.

Iron determination

Iron salts are present in **surface and ground waters** – their natural concentration depends on geological structure and hydrological conditions of the river basin. High iron content in surface waters indicates water pollution with industrial or mine wastewater, especially wastewater coming from metalworking plants, etching works, etc.

The presence of iron in water can be determined with the help of two procedures that require adding reagents to the water sample and analysis of an evaporated residuum. In the first case, 10 ml of a water sample is poured into a test-tube, then one drop of aquafortis (concentrated nitric acid), several drops of 5% solution of hydrogen peroxide and about 0.5 ml of 20% solution of potassium thiocyanate are added. If iron content is about 0.1 mg/l then a light pink coloration of the solution will appear. If iron content in water sample is higher, a red color will appear.

The other procedure is as follows: If a dry yellow or light yellow residuum is left in the cup after water evaporation, then iron salts can be discovered with the help of solutions of potassium ferricyanide as well as potassium or ammonium thiocyanate. The appearance of blue residuum caused by potassium ferricyanide as well as a blood red color caused by ammonium thiocyanate indicates presence of iron ions.

Chlorides (salts of hydrochloric acid) are detected according to water cloudiness when adding silver nitrate or lead nitrate (0.1 mole/l) with subsequent cooling of the test-tube under a stream of cold water.

It is advised to determine **hydrocarbonates** (acid salts of carbonic acid) if the pH of the test water sample is equal or more than 7. A solution of hydrochloric acid is added drop by drop to the test water sample. An intensive, odorless bubbling indicates the presence of hydrocarbonates.

If the solution of hydrochloric acid is added to the residuum that has been cooled after evaporation, and boiling with bubble-formation is observed, this means that it is hydrocarbonate water. If the solution does not boil, it means that it contains calcium or magnesium sulfates and chlorides.

If water tastes salty or bitter/salty then dry residuum can be analyzed for the presence of sodium or potassium salts. It can be done as follows: Put some dry residuum on a tip of a knife made of stainless steel and then bring it into an outer cone of torch flame. A yellow flame indicates the presence of **sodium salts**, whereas a lilac-violet color will reveal presence of **potassium salts**, and a brick-red color, the presence of **calcium salts**.

Determination of phenols

Phenols are aromatic chemical compounds with one or several hydroxyl groups attached directly to a benzene ring, for instance, *phenol, cresols, thymol, chlorophenols and nitrophenols*. If their concentration is about several milligrams per 1 liter, they can exert influence upon the biological life of water bodies. Some phenols (if their concentration is about several micrograms per 1 liter) cause objectionable chlorophenol odor and taste, which appears after chlorination of surface waters in the course of drinking water disinfection.

In order to detect the presence of phenols in water, 100 ml of a test sample is poured into a beaker flask of 200 ml and then a solution of bleaching powder or chlorine water is added to the sample so that 0.05 mg of active chlorine is added. A characteristic "pharmaceutical" smell of chlorophenols is checked in 10 minutes at 20 and 60 degrees Celsius (see procedure of smell determination).

Some quantitative chemical analyses

Any quantitative chemical analyses, i.e. analyses that produce data on content (quantity) of a chemical substance in water, require expensive equipment, chemical knowledge, accuracy in test procedure compliance. Therefore, they can be performed by students only in conditions of a **well-equipped chemical laboratory** under supervision of a chemistry teacher. Thus, at the present lesson we recommend not to go deep into qualitative measurements, but to use numerous test-kits that allow you to determine roughly both qualitative and some quantitative properties of water. First of all, they include such parameters as acidity (pH), and the concentration of nitrates, ammonium, oxygen and carbon dioxide.

Test-kits for all mentioned substances are sold at aquarium supply stores. We will briefly describe most widespread chemical analyses of great importance in ecological studies in the given section.

Water acidity (content of hydrogen ions or pH)

Acidity or pH of water indicates whether it is acidic or alkaline water, and is measured in the range of 0 to 14. The value of 7 is neutral

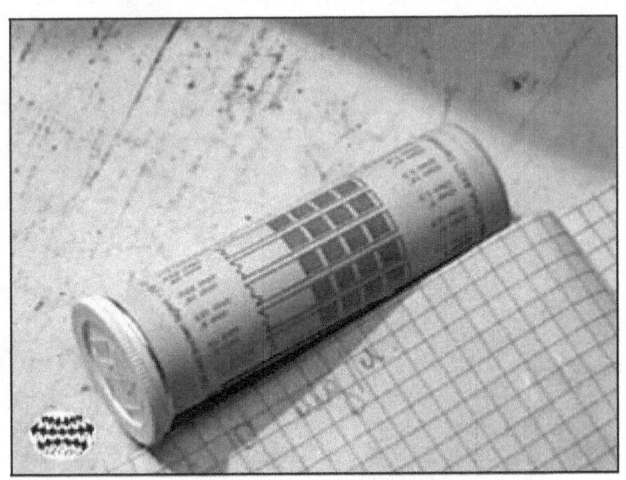

according to scale of acidity, from 6 to 0 – acidic, and from 8 to 15 – alkaline.

Stagnant (swamp) water is usually acidic (4 - 5) due to the presence of organic acids, whereas normal clean water has pH value close to neutral (6.5 – 8.5). It is accepted that pH values from 5.5. to 8.5 are optimal for development of aquatic organisms.

An abrupt change of pH in a water body can lead to the dilution of some substances in water and poisoning of aquatic organisms. If pH values suddenly change and become more acidic or alkaline, special attention should be paid to possible industrial discharge.

As far as precipitation acidity concerns, clean rainwater and clean snow have pH value 5.6 – it is slightly more acid than the pH value of distilled water (pH=7). It happens as easily soluble carbon dioxide is always present in air. When it combines with water, it forms carbonic acid, which acidifies atmospheric precipitates. If there are many nitrogen oxides, sulfur dioxide (SO_4) and other acidic substances present in the air, then pH values of snow or rainwater will be less than 5.6. If the pH value of snow is higher than 5.6 then it is alkaline and it is most likely polluted with metal oxides and/or automobile exhaust gases (aromatic hydrocarbons).

It is easier to determine pH with the help of indicator bands with different measuring ranges, which are produced in many countries. However, this method is the least accurate one of all the test methods; its accuracy is 0.5 - 1.

Liquid test-kits provide best results, where several drops of a chemical reagent are added to the test water sample, and the water color obtained is compared to the provided color scale. The accuracy of such tests is up to 0.2 – 0.5.

Determination of dissolved oxygen

Dissolved oxygen content is one of the most important biological properties of water as it indicates the presence of organic substances in water and serves as an evidence of respiration and decay in the body of water.

Low oxygen content indicates a large inflow of organic substances into water, for instance, from stock-farms or sewage discharge. Oxygen content in water also depends on water temperature. It has also been revealed that the oxygen content in water is dependent upon photosynthesis. The more plants that are found in water, the higher the oxygen content during daylight time, while less at night. Considerable diurnal variation is registered, which also has to be taken into account when taking water samples.

The European Commission on Environmental Conservation set the maximum acceptable level of dissolved oxygen content as 4 mg/l. Indices below the mentioned value indicate pollution of the water body.

As for most qualitative analyses, the simplest method of oxygen content measurement is an analysis with the help of test-kits or an instrument called an oxygen-meter.

Presentation of results

This activity should result in a table of comparative data on water properties in different natural water bodies, artificial water sources and properties of snow in the vicinity of the school or field study center. The number of studied parameters and sources is not regulated according to the given educational task, as it depends on availability of test-kits, equipment and chemical reagents, as well as on the presence of water sources.

Results obtained for different sources should be compared and

students should try to reveal the causes of found differences: why a specific water-body is characterized with specific properties of water. What determines snow and rainwater properties in different locations?

If any material resources (test-kits, chemical reagents and instruments) are lacking, the activity can be focused on analysis of physical properties of water taken from different sources (the more, the better) and on making a map of snow cover pollution with suspended particles.

The study of water invertebrates in a local river and assessment of its environmental state

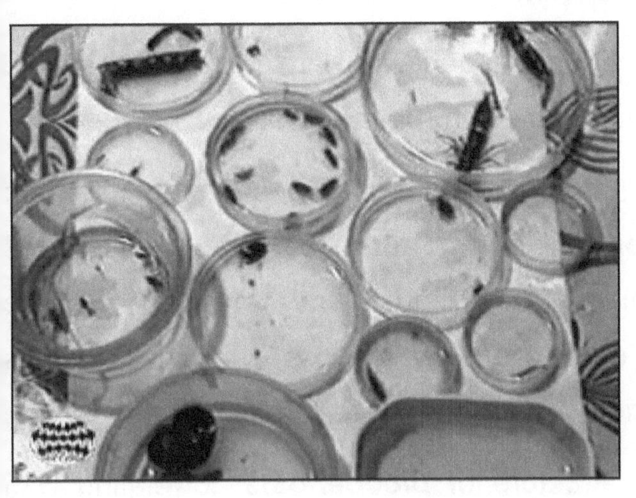

This manual is devoted to the study of macrozoobenthos - invertebrates that inhabit the bottom of bodies of water. The main idea of this lesson is to study these invertebrates in a local small river or stream and to determine water quality based on species composition and representation of various collected organisms.

Introduction

Zoobenthos (from bentos – depth) all the invertebrates that inhabit the bottom of bodies of water (or the **benthic** zone), aquatic vegetation (or **phytal**) as well as other substrates including those associated with **hydroengineering** facilities.

The largest benthic specimens, with a body size of more than 2 mm, are called **macrozoobenthos**. The following make up the category Macrozoobenthos: worms (**planaria, oligochaetae**, *leeches, round worms*), **mollusks** (**gastropoda and bivalves**), **Crustacea** class (**amphipods, isopods, decapods**, etc), **arachnids**, and insects (*midges, **geleides**, May-flies, stoneflies, caddis-flies, dragon flies* and so on), etc.

Many of these living organisms also dwell in the water column (**pelagic** zone); they include insects, **Crustacea** class (**mysidacea, pallacea** and others), *spiders*, etc.

The lives of many other bottom organisms can also be connected with the water surface, i.e. surface film (**neistalic** zone).

According to its functions, macrozoobenthos represents an important part of the **heterotrophic component of water systems**. Macrozoobenthic organisms are particularly involved in the processes of converting outside energy sources (plant and detritus material) into available energy within the system.

Changes in the species structure of *biocoenosis* correlating with level of water pollution have attracted **hydrobiologists'** attention for a long time. The high **stenobionicty** (demands for certain environmental conditions) of a number of species, formation of complex multi-component systems, attachment to certain types of substrates, relative low motility (mobility) (in comparison with fast-spreading pollutants) allow the use of zoobenthic organisms as indicators for determining human (**anthropogeneous**) impact on aqueous ecosystems.

Different methods of water quality assessment, numerous articles and publications as well as the data of long-term observations within the hydrological network of environmental monitoring prove the importance of benthos for determining characteristics of water quality. Because macrozoobenthos specimens are relatively large, their detection and determination by young ecologists (environmentalists) is made easier.

Procedure for studying macrozoobenthos

General information

The study of macrozoobenthos and fulfillment of this educational task can best be carried out at a **nearby small river or stream** with a slow current.

An ideal location for studying zoobenthos is a river valley, which is not too wide (5-20 meters wide) and not too deep (up to 1.5 meters deep), or a relatively flat section of a mountain river with a slow flow and well-developed high aqueous vegetation. A fast mountain river

with a coarse-silted bottom and absence of high aqueous vegetation, or reservoirs with stagnant water are less suitable for this research.

In order to make sample collection easier it is recommended to choose a shallow river section to collect samples at different places by walking in the river (not from a boat or a bridge). Periods of sample collections are limited by the **seasonal life cycles** of benthic organisms. These life cycles occur year round and are not limited to the period from July to November.

Sample collection

Selection of sites for sampling in the river is the starting point of all hydrobiological studies.

For the purposes of this task, an **average river section** should be chosen. The best area will have favorable oxygen conditions, such as shade and high water vegetation. It is not advisable to collect samples at where ground water discharges, at stagnant sections, or other unfavorable river sites. These areas will not give a true indication of the entire river system.

Samples collected from the *abyssal* part of a river are also not suitable, because they may not characterize water quality but rather, the pollution of bottom sedimentation, which can greatly differ in chemical composition from the water in the river as whole.

For these studies, mountain and piedmont rivers with rocky-pebbled bottoms are best. If these conditions are unattainable, (or for river valleys) samples should be collected from submerged *macrophytes* (high water plants). If there are no enumerated substrates, or in the case of a water level increase, samples should be collected from the merged *terricole* or submerged vegetation. If such vegetation is also not present, then samples are collected from soft soils – sand, clay and silt.

To conclude this section, we can once again outline that samples according to the objectives of this lesson should be collected **in average** (on all parameters) river sections and, certainly, **in different parts** of the river.

Sampling technique

The most convenient and universal tool of macrozoobenthos collection is a scraper, which is a metal frame with a cutting edge with attached gauze or netted bag placed on a stick (also known as a D-net.)

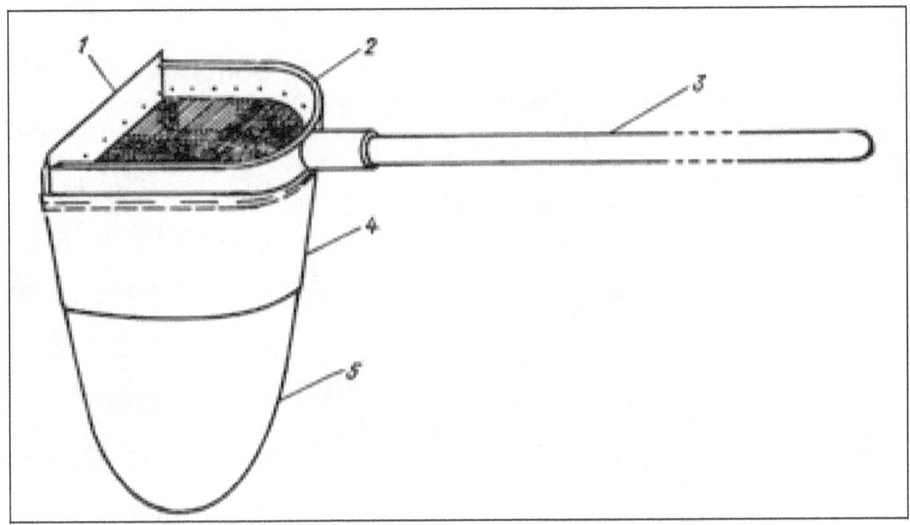

Figure 1: Scraper: 1 – cutting edge; 2 – frame; 3 – handle; 4 – cotton fabric part of the washing sieve; 5 – part of the sieve made of kapron.

The scraper allows the student investigator to collect both **qualitative and quantitative samples from all types of substrates**, including such specific substrates as the submerged overgrown sides of *ferries, walls of hydroengineering facilities, bridge piles* and so on.

The sampling technique using a scraper has some peculiarities. When collecting samples in the river, the scraper should first be placed down the **watercourse** (downstream) from the substrate from which the samples are to be collected. In that case, organisms together with suspended soil particles or substrate fragments will fall into the scraper's screen with the water current. In fast rivers, stir the bottom with a foot; a person should move with one side forward and place the scraper downstream.

On rocky substrates the organisms should first be washed into the scrape with a gentle movement of a hand from the rock surface, then the scraper should be turned upside down and it should smooth the bottom surface.

When a large cluster of algae or macrophytes fall into the scraper, without taking them out of the screen they should be shaken in the water and then removed. Large pebbles that fall into the screen should be removed after the screen is carefully examined and all organisms are taken out with the help of forceps.

When samples are collected from plant thickets and filamentous algae, they should be shaken in the screen of the scraper, submerged into the water and then they should be once again examined in order to collect attached organisms. When collecting samples from dense thickets of microphytes, the scraper should be pushed into the thicket; then the thicket should be "mowed" with sharp, energetic movements.

After each collection of samples, the scraper should be taken out of the water and its contents should be put carefully into a container or a dishpan filled with clean water from the river. The screen should be turned inside out. All organisms seen with the naked eye should be collected (with fingers, with the help of pincers (forceps), a spoon, etc. – depending on the size) and placed into a glass container with a wide neck for sample storage and transportation to the field center. Due to active movements even small organisms are well seen in a white pan. NOTE: Specimens can be separated in the field (old ice cube trays work well), identified and counted if they are to be returned directly to the water.

When collecting samples from sandy, soft clayey bottoms or silt the scraper is immersed into the bottom several centimeters deep and the bottom surface layer is cut out with a cutting edge with a scraping movement. The scraper's movements are directed up the watercourse. The method of *elutriation* is applied for sampling from

such substrates. First, soil collected in the scraper is washed out directly in the scraper, which is immersed several times and taken out of the water, and then is transported to a bucket or a bowl with water. Then the soil is stirred several times with a rotary movement. Suspended particles together with organisms are poured into a previously rinsed scraper after each stirring and then into a pan or a container with clean water. Taking into account the low inhabitance of sandy bottoms, this operation should be repeated several times. In order to avoid rubbing the organisms with coarse sand particles and other trauma, the stirring should be done carefully with smooth, gentle movements.

For the purposes of this lesson, all organisms collected at different river sites can be placed into the same glass jar.

Accompanying description of the river and samples

Before starting to collect benthos samples, the **riverside zone should be examined**. All soils should be observed at about 50 meters up the watercourse and 50 meters down. The typical appearance of the riverside zone should be recorded directly at the sampling site and a map of the area sketched. In addition the student researchers should record: 1) number of the sample, 2) date and time of sampling, 3) name of the river, 4) location of sampling site (map).

The following **information** should also be provided: 1) water and air temperature at the time of sample collection, 2) weather conditions on the day of sampling and during previous days (retrospective information on weather conditions helps to explain the occurrence of possible abnormal findings). It is advisable to record a visual description of hydrological parameters of the river in the field register: 1) stream velocity, 2) color, 3) water transparency, 5) degree of the riverbed filling.

In order to make recording easier data can be recorded on the **Exploratory Description Form** (Table 3 at the end of this manual).

Information concerning the benthos itself should include: 1) substrate, where the samples were collected from, 2) distance from the bank, 3) depth of sampling site, 4) number of scraping movements (one scraping movement is a conventional unit of sampling area expressed in distance covered by the scraper in the bottom.) It is convenient, for example, to move a distance of 50 cm in a soft bottom (which is covered with a cutting edge) for one "scraping movement." In this case, the width of the cutting edge should be recorded as well. The description of the river is concluded with "notes, "where observations of life in the biocoenosis (such as first flight of insects, abundance of empty shells of mollusks, unformed state of the biocoenosis, etc.) are recorded.

Sample processing and species determination

Analysis and species determination should be carried out during the same day, while the organisms are still alive. After returning to the lab, the samples from the glass containers are poured out into white pans filled with, preferably, water from the same river (two to

three liters of water should be brought from the river in a bottle).

Then all collected organisms are sorted into Petri dishes. Organisms of the same species (at least according to their appearance) are placed in one dish.

The collected animals are **identified** using field guides or other visual/descriptive keys. A binocular microscope may be helpful. It is advisable that each student gets training in species determination and draws at least one organism.

When determination is finished, a total list of collected organisms is written. It is not necessary to determine correct species name; it is important to register the presence or absence of the main **indicative** groups of organisms, which will be used later for the assessment of environmental status of the river.

Assessment of the environmental state of the river based on biological index

The biological index method of estimation developed by F. **Woodiwiss** in 1964 is the most widely used method within the system of environmental monitoring. It applies the evaluation of water quality according to zoobenthos parameters.

The method is based on a relationship of simplification of **biocoenosis** taxonomic structure in correlation with an increase of **water pollution level** (owing to the absence of indicative taxons at achieving their tolerance limits) with a simultaneous decrease of diversity of organisms that belong to the "Woodiwiss's groups" (Table 1):

Each species of flatworm	Fly larvae (except midges and buffalo gnats)
Oligochaetae class (except Nais genus)	Midges (except *Chironomus thummi*)
Nais genus	Beetles
Each species of leeche	Alder and snake flies
Mollusks	Each family of caddis-flies
Crustacea class	Buffalo gnats
Stoneflies	Bugs
Mayflies	Larva of *Chironomus thummi*

When calculating the total number of Woodiwiss's groups, the presence of at least one specimen from the specified groups in the sample accounts for one point.

Among these 16 groups of organisms, Woodiwiss determined six indicative taxons. The presence of these taxons in the studied reservoir, together with presence of other animals (biodiversity of the benthic community), indicates degree of reservoir purity (Table 2). These groups were identified on the basis of a large database collected by the author.

According to this method, there is no necessity to determine exact species – the determination should be limited by the taxon specified in the table. For some of the taxons (*mayflies, stoneflies, caddis-flies*), only the fact of their species presence or absence is taken into account. Attitude to different species is determined visually according to organism appearance.

The presence of at least one specimen of the corresponding taxon is considered as its presence in the water body.

The working scale for calculation of biological index based on the presence of Woodiwiss's groups is given in Table 2:

Indicative taxons	Species diversity	Number of Woodiwiss's groups in the sample				
		0-1	2-5	6-10	11-15	16+
Stonefly larvae	More than one species	-	7	8	9	10
	Only one species	-	6	7	8	9
Mayfly larvae*	More than one species	-	6	7	8	9
	Only one species	-	5	6	7	8
Caddis-fly larvae **	More than one species	-	5	6	7	8
	Only one species	-	4	5	6	7
Gammarus	All above listed taxons are absent	3	4	5	6	7
Hog slater	Same	2	3	4	5	6
Tubiphicides and Chiromonuseae larvae	Same	1	2	3	4	-
All above listed taxons are absent	Some organisms which require lower oxygen levels can be present	0	1	2	-	-

*- Except *Baetis rhodani*
** - Including *Baetis rhodani*

When working with the table:

One should move from the top to the bottom of the left column of the table, determining if the indicative organism marked in the column is in the sample. The first organism found in your sample will be indicative – it will determine the degree of water purity. Then it is not necessary to move further down the table.

If some stoneflies, mayflies or caddis-flies are present in your sample then you must determine if you have only one species or several (according to their appearance).

If none of the stoneflies, Mayflies or caddis-flies are present in the sample then you have to move further down the table until you meet some indicative organisms which are present in your sample.

Calculate the number of Woodiwiss's groups in the sample (according to Table 1). Find the value of the biological index where the line of found diversity crosses the column of the number of Woodiwiss's groups, which corresponds to your sample.

This will be your indicator of relative water quality (purity) in the river – biological index. The higher the index is, the cleaner the water is. Biological index is a relative indicator and is measured from 0 (very dirty water) up to 10 (pure water).

Example:

Assume that two species of flatworms were found in the sample (they present two Woodiwiss's groups according to Table 1), as well as several species of Oligochaetae (all Oligochaetae species belong to one group), three species of leeches (3 groups), mollusks (1 group), Crustacea class (1), several species of mayflies (1), bugs (1), fly larvae (1), one family of caddis-flies (1) and Alder and snake flies (1).

We estimate number of Woodiwiss's groups (using Table 1); in our case it is equal to 13.

Then we find the "highest" taxon according to Table 2. It is mayflies (there are no stoneflies in the sample). We have several species, so we take the upper line. At the crossing of this line with the column "11-15," we find the biological index of our water body to be 8.

Presentation of results

A **consolidated table should be compiled** based on study results. The title of this table is "Macrozoobenthic organisms of the river and results of assessment of water purity according to indicative taxons."

The list of found organisms (taxons at the level of Woodiwiss's groups) lays the basis for the consolidated table together with drawings of each taxon (various species can also be shown).

At the top of the table, indicative **taxons** (from Table 2) should be 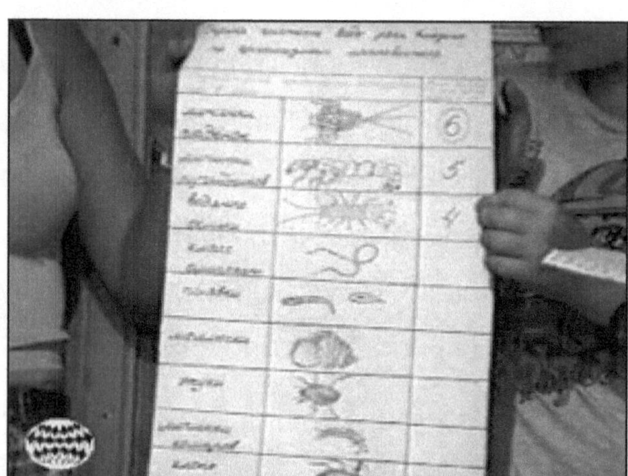 recorded starting from the highest and then other organisms that belong to Woodiwiss's groups (from Table 1) and at the bottom of the table, a list of found species that do not belong to Woodiwiss's groups.

To the right against the names and drawings of the indicative organisms, corresponding biological indexes should be filled in (from Table 2). The highest (and maximum according to the index) will characterize the degree of relative purity of water in the studied river.

Additional information on river description and data on sample collection (it is recommended to mark sampling sites on a map of the river) should be supplied as an Appendix to the main table.

Woodiwiss, F.S., The Biological system of stream classification used by the Trent River Board, Chem. and Ind., 1964, vol. 11, pp. 433-447.

Table 3.

Exploratory Description Form for a Water Body № ______

1. Date of observation _____________________________ (day, month, year)
2. Weather conditions ____
   (air temperature, cloudiness, wind strength, precipitation, snow cover and ice)
3. Type and name of the water body_____________________________________
4. Location of the studied area (observation site)___________________________

____
   (administrative district where the observation site is located and its distance from the nearest human settlement)
5. Vicinity description (description of the surrounding environment) _____

____
   (village, town, city, forest, meadows, agricultural lands, etc. and their short description)
6. Morphometrical features of the site _______________________________

____
   (width, average depth, stream velocity, shore type, slope of the bottom)
7. Riverside water vegetation (dominant species)________________________

____
8. High aquatic vegetation (dominant species) __________________________

____
9. Description of the river bottom soil and shore soils __________________

____
   (stone type, stone-sand type, sandy soil, silt-sandy type, sand-silty type, silty type, clay type)
10. General description of water:
a) water temperature: near a bank ________ , far from a bank ________ ,
at a depth of 1 m ________ b) water color _________________________
   (blue, green, yellow-green, green-yellow, yellow, brown-yellow, or brown)
c) water transparency ____
   (technique of measurement – Sekki disc/glass cylinder)
d) water smell

____
   (its presence or absence, description and strength)
11. Characteristics of growth on underwater objects (periphyton) ________

(color, shape and size)

12. Water surface pollution _______________________________________

(oil film, spots, foam, different floating objects, algae gatherings, etc. and their extend)

13. Fauna of the water body and its vicinity _______________________

(water invertebrates, insects flying above the water surface, fish, birds, etc.)

14. Main types of human impact _________________________________

____

____

(industrial, household and agricultural sources of pollution: presence, intensity and distance from the studied area)

Authors of the description _______________________________________

Study of plankton

This manual contains procedures for studying meso- and microzooplankton in freshwater bodies, including techniques of sampling, sample conservation, qualitative and quantitative analyses. Emphasis is on long term studies using identical field study techniques. Variations and options for additional studies are described.

Introduction

The **zooplankton community** is one of the main components of water-body *biocenosis*.

The term "*plankton*" comes from the Greek word meaning "hover." Thus, zooplankton is a group of rather small animals drifting in the water column. Plankton is abundant in lakes, ponds and reservoirs. Its biomass and populations are significantly lower in rivers.

The zooplankton community, as any other community in an ecosystem, is characterized by a constancy of species diversity, dynamic stability and a certain structure peculiar to the plankton community.

Change in water conditions causes changes in the proportions of plankton and other water animals. Sometimes it is possible to make a conclusion on the possible cause of changes, based on their analysis: excessive increase of fish populations, changes in the chemical composition of water (for instance, acidification), and so on. That is why **long-term and repeated** (in the course of a year) observations of plankton are of particular interest in ecological studies.

Most procedures for assessing any parameters of a body of water based on a single series of sampling do not stand up to critique. For example, if you go to the Sahara desert in spring and carry out a one-time survey, then you can make a conclusion that environmental conditions in the region are favorable for fruit growing: it is very warm there in spring and there is enough moisture. However, a dry season will come in a month and the desert will become barren.

Thus, studies of plankton that have been conducted within a week are of no interest to scientists: they provide information only on the given week of the year, but they do not give an idea of the structure and functioning of the community as a whole.

Long-term studies should be carried out in the course of a long period of time and according to the same technique, otherwise, results of studies obtained in different years cannot be compared and variability trends cannot be revealed.

Techniques for plankton collection

It is ideal to **collect and count the individual plankton** animals. This is rather difficult due to the large differences in their sizes: from 20 microns to several millimeters. This manual describes methods for census of **mesoplankton** (1mm and larger), which include *Daphnia,*

Polyphemus and others, *and* **microplankton** (50 – 1000 microns) – larvae of **Copepods** (*nautilus* and *copepodites*), **water fleas** *Bosmina, Diaphanosoma,* and *rotifers*. The sampling method depends on the type of water body, its depth and size.

Sampling with the help of a plankton net

Construction of a plankton net. A plankton net is a net made of a special cloth called "plankton gauze," which lets water pass, but collects plankton. The net also has a container to collect animals that are accumulated in the course of sampling (filtering) (Picture 1a).

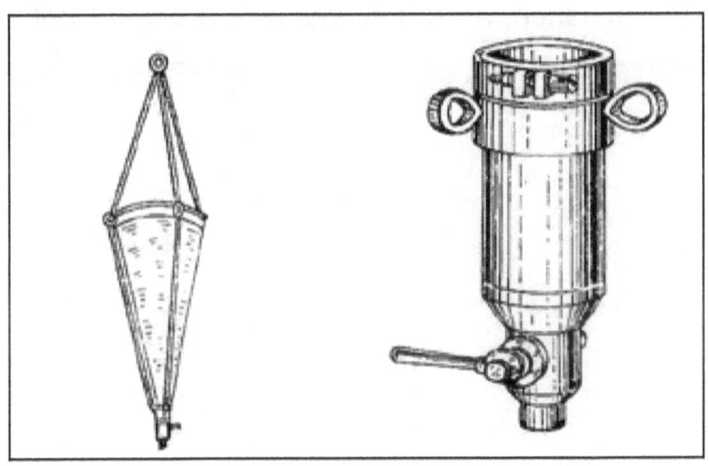

Picture. 1: a – a plankton net, b – a plankton glass

The plankton net can be homemade. You will need a mill sieve (with cells of 0.15 – 0.1 mm), several pieces of wire, tight cloth and a plankton glass (Picture 1b).

You can use parachute kapron instead of "plankton gauze," but do not use cotton medical gauze as it is too soft and it has cells that are too big.

The cloth is cut out in the form of a cone and sewn to a metal hoop at its upper part and to a plankton glass at its lower part. In both cases, the "gauze" should not be sewed directly to the hoop or glass, but to a band of cloth (flax, coarse calico or cotton), otherwise it will be too easily torn where it joins together.

Two standard size plankton nets are used in hydrobiological monitoring – with a diameter of the inlet – 25 or 40cm and length of the cone – 55 or 100 cm correspondingly.

A commercial plankton glass can be replaced by any glass or plastic containers (for instance, an empty vial with a cut out bottom), with a

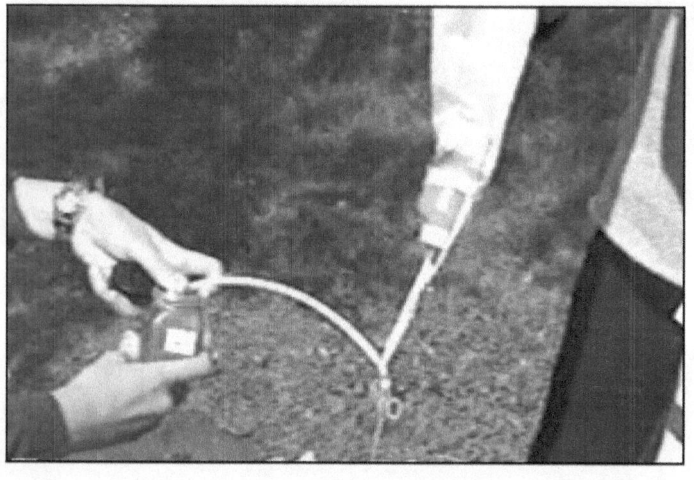

discharge device at the bottom (for instance, it is possible to put a rubber tube with a tube clamp on a bottle neck, or an outlet can just be plugged with a rubber plug). The junction of the glass (bottle) and the net is sewed around with cloth.

Main techniques for using a plankton net are creeping and filtering

Creeping

When using a method of creeping in hydrobiological studies, it is recommended to take three samples with the help of a plankton net by catching and filtering a horizon of 0-10 m. Samples are taken from a boat once a month.

If the depth of the water body is less than 10m, then creeping should be carried out from the bottom up to water surface, trying not to put the net on the bottom, because in that case, mud and benthic organisms will come into the net (benthic organisms are not plankton).

While sweeping, if you know the hoop diameter, you can estimate the volume of swept water column ($V = r\,h$).

In order to determine the depth of sampling, it is necessary to make marks every meter on the string used for creeping. For instance, you can make knots or sew colored ribbons or braids.

Filtering

In order to filter water, it is scooped up with a container of a known volume (such as a bucket). Water samples are **"condensed"** by

pouring water into the neck of a plankton net. All the water from the bucket runs out through the walls of the plankton net cone, whereas the desired plankton forms sediment in the plankton net.

It is possible to **calculate the volume** of filtered water if you know the volume of one bucket and the number of poured buckets.

The volume of "filtered" water depends on zooplankton numbers and varies within the range of 10 (in rich water bodies in summer) up to 300 (in winter) liters. In any case, quantitative samples are brought to a standard volume in calculations (for instance, 1 liter).

Filtering technique is especially important and it is often used in studies of coastal plankton, as its species composition differs from the species composition in the center of the water body.

Layer-by-layer sampling with the help of a bathometer

Bathometers are devices of different constructions designed for water sampling at different depths. The classical bathometer is a cylinder,

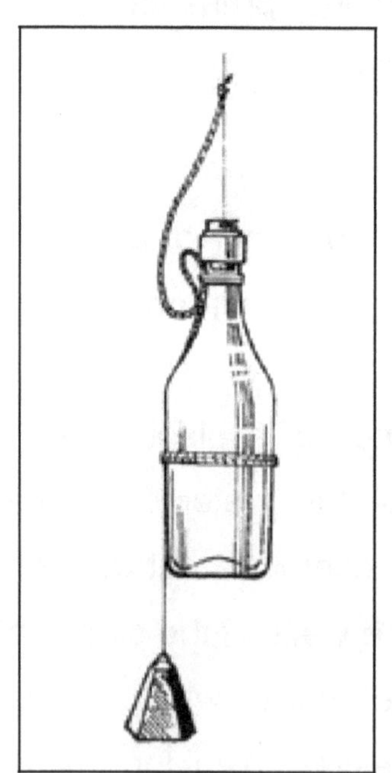

which can be immersed at a certain depth. It is then closed and taken out together with its contents. Unfortunately it is not easy to make a classical bathometer.

A glass bottle with a narrow neck and wooden plug, which is made heavier with a weight, can be used as a simple bathometer. The bigger the bottle, the better. Two strings are tied to the bottle: one is attached to the bottleneck and one to the plug (Picture 2: Self-made bathometer).

When the bottle is submerged to a desired depth (the weight is necessary to make sure it sinks), you should abruptly pull the plug out (do not plug the bottle tightly beforehand), and in a minute or two, pull the bottle out of the water as quickly as possible. If the pulling speed fast enough and the bottleneck is narrow, water from superincumbent layers does not enter the bottle.

Samples that have been brought to the surface with the help of a bathometer should also be "condensed" by using a plankton net (as described above). Then volume of filtered water is calculated.

As it is recommended to have a large volume of "filtered" water (if possible), then the bathometer should be made as big as possible – for instance, you can use a two-liter glass or plastic bottle or any other vessel of a bigger size with a narrow neck.

In order to determine the depth of sample, it is also recommended to make marks on the string for each meter. The string is then attached to the bottle.

If a bathometer or any substituting container is available, then it is possible to trace daily migrations of zooplankton from the depth to the surface and back.

Scheme of sampling

While carrying out serious hydrobiological studies, **sampling should be conducted routinely in the course of year** – usually twice a month. However, the following schedule of sampling can be suggested in order to obtain approximate data (this schedule was designed for Central Russia – it can be modified for any area):

1st sampling: beginning of May (beginning of increase in numbers of different living organisms).

2nd sampling: end of May (Peak of population size of Copepods subclass and their larvae);

3rd sampling: beginning/middle of June (peak of Daphnia's' population size);

4th sampling: end of June (overgrowing the water body, depression of zooplankton, development of small forms);

5th ,6th,and 7th sampling – one sampling in each of the following months: July, August, and September;

8th sampling: October (at this time it is possible to find male Cladocera, which can be easily identified up to species name).

Distribution of points, where samples are taken on the same day is usually carried out along a certain axis. One sample is taken in the middle of the water body, the second sample is taken halfway to the shore and the third one is taken near the bank. Samples are usually taken in the morning when there is no wind and the water surface is calm.

Numbers of plankton organisms are usually quite low in winter, especially in the period of ice until the thaw. Rather interesting events take place in early spring, but sampling should be carried out very carefully. Ice becomes fragile and it is difficult to step on it, but it is still impossible to use a boat. In rivers, the amount of plankton is very low, therefore, it is recommended to take samples in bays or areas of low velocity, where the plankton are more abundant.

Preserving and labeling samples

Temporary storage of samples

When creeping or filtering is over, water accumulated in the plankton glass together with settled zooplankton (which is the desired "sample") is carefully poured into a clean container of corresponding volume. The container should be rinsed twice with "local" water beforehand. Any glass and plastic vials, small bottles, etc (about 50-200ml) with hermetically screwed caps can be used as containers for the temporary storage of samples.

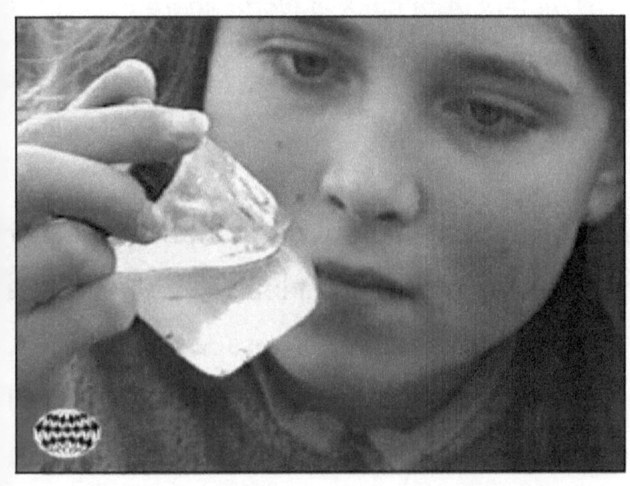

A vial with a temporarily stored sample (before coming to the lab) is wrapped in paper, where the necessary notes on the date, place and time of sampling are taken down (see below).

Collected samples are immediately examined (living forms) or fixed in the lab depending on the purpose of the study.

Prior to fixation, samples can be diluted or condensed – excess water can be pumped out with the help of a "closed pipette," i.e. a pipette, with the suction opening covered with plankton gauze.

Samples are usually fixed with formalin on the basis of calculations in order to obtain a 4% solution. Formalin is usually a 40% solution, so you will have to take one part of formalin per nine parts of water sample. However, fixed samples should be kept in a warm place, as formalin forms much sediment at temperatures below zero. If formalin is not available, a 70% alcohol solution can be used.

Each sample to be stored or to be further transported should have a label. The label should contain the following information (example):

Sample number:	*18/1*
Body of Water:	*Lake Mary, Near Flagstaff Arizona*
Date:	*June 5, 2002*
Sampling place:	*10 meters from dock at North shore*
Depth (horizon):	*0 -10 m*
Catching instrument :	*Plankton net*

The **label** should be written in India ink on parchment paper or tracing paper and put inside the vial, where samples will be kept. It is advised to organize registration of all samples in a special field log, where you write down the time of sampling, its serial number as well as all the information stated on the label. It is also advisable to take down an hour of sampling (as plankton organisms are characterized by having daily migrations) and meteorological data: air temperature and water temperature measured at the surface, cloudiness, wind force, etc.

Sample processing

Qualitative processing

Qualitative processing of samples is aimed at the determination of **species composition** of the living organisms forming plankton. Identification of some animals can be carried out only while organisms are alive, so along with fixed samples, it is necessary to take several "living" qualitative samples, which should be examined immediately on return to the laboratory.

Glassware that is used for work with living and fixed samples should be separated, as even insignificant traces of formalin or alcohol can kill living organisms.

Part of the sample from a vial, into which water with plankton was poured after creeping (filtering), is transferred by a pipette into a small vessel (for instance, a Petri dish), where it is examined under a

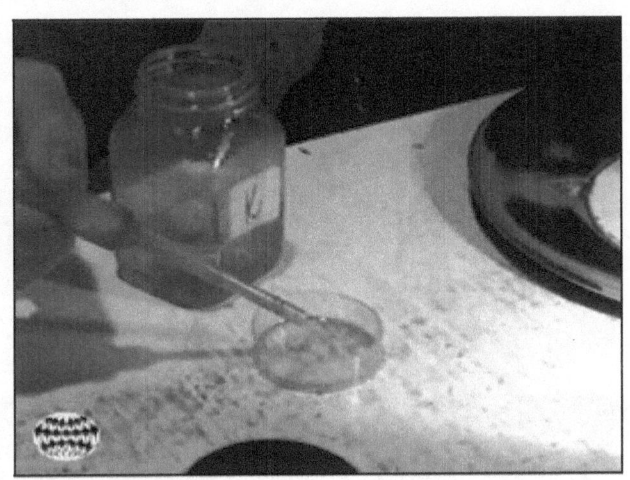

binocular microscope at low magnification. Separate specimens are caught by a pipette and placed on the object-plate in order to be examined under high magnification or under a compound microscope. When examining them under a microscope, a well slide may be necessary for larger organisms. Movement of living organisms under a cover glass becomes slower or stops, which is convenient for identifying species. Adding a viscous substance, for example, starch aster, can also slow movements down.

Organisms that do not require their identification while they are alive can be examined and identified by extracting them out of fixed samples with a pipette. Part of the sample is also put into a Petri dish, then single specimens are taken out for identification. Glycerin can be added to the drop of liquid on the slide in order to increase transparency. Identification is carried out according to field guides and keys.

Quantitative processing of samples

The objective of quantitative processing is the **estimation of the numbers of different animal species within the sample and the whole body of water**. If there are few animals in the sample, then all of them are counted in the whole sample ("few" organisms means a number of specimens which can be counted, i.e. not more than a hundred). Contents of the sample are condensed and poured into a special counting chamber.

Two types of counting chambers are common.

1) Goryaev's chamber is a small vessel with incisions in the form of squares (sides are of a certain length, for instance, 1cm) on the bottom. All of the sample or its part of known volume (use a

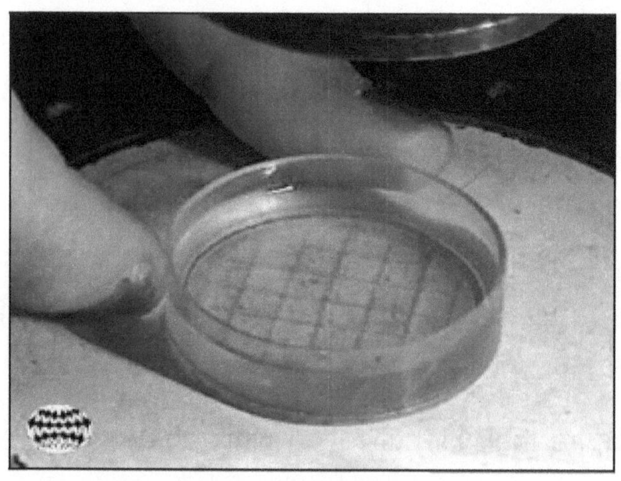

volumetric pipette – see below) is poured into the counting chamber and then the chamber is placed under a binocular microscope.

It is quite easy to make such a chamber on your own: take a plastic (disposable) Petri dish and line (harrow) a grid in which each square has a side of 1cm length. Scratches on a glass Petri dish can be made with the help of a scalpel's tip, a preparation needle, etc.

Squares of the grid should be numbered on the reverse side of the Petri dish. In order to make a grid of squares so that the numbers are well seen, ink is poured over the bottom of the dish is or the dish is painted over with a marker. The paint is wiped off, but it will remain in the scratches.

After you have counted a number of specimens of each species in several squares (or even in all of them), you can estimate a total number of specimens of each species in the sample. Because the volume of the water, which has been caught through with a plankton net, is known (see above), then the number of specimens of the given species in one liter of water can be easily calculated: Nav = Nsam / Vwat, where Nav is the average number of specimens of the given species in one liter of water taken from the water body; Nsam is the number of specimens of the species in the sample, and Vwat is the volume of caught water in liters.

2) Bogorov's chamber is more convenient for the estimation of

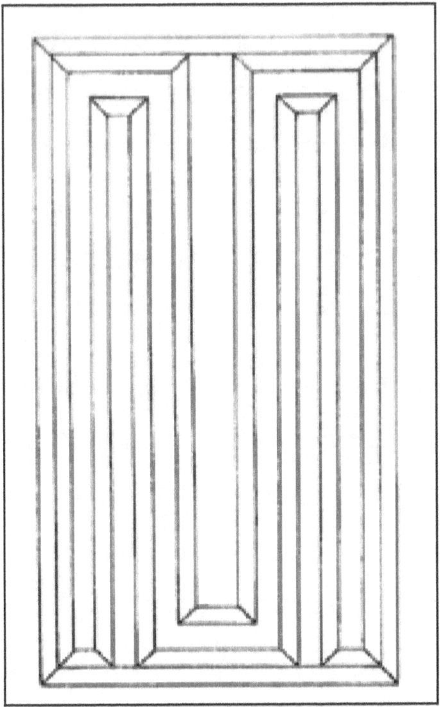

"thick" samples, which contain many specimens. It is a thick glass or Plexiglas plate with a groove in the form of a labyrinth (Picture 3: Bogorov's chamber). Bogorov's chamber can also be made without any assistance. An ideal technique for making a chamber is to use a thick (1cm) piece of Plexiglas with the help of a milling cutter (up to 0.5 cm). If a milling cutter is not available, then a labyrinth can be glued out of Plexiglas bands.

Labyrinth grooves should not be wider than 0.5 cm in order to make sure that all water with animals fits a binocular visual field at 20-30-times magnification (it is usually enough to carry out quantitative estimations).

Labyrinth grooves should be 0.5-1 cm deep. Length of the labyrinth is not important and it is usually about 40-44cm (four "curves" of 10cm each).

The whole sample is poured into the chamber, then the chamber is placed under a binocular microscope so that the field of view follows along the labyrinth from its beginning to its end. At the same time all animals found in the field of vision are counted. Then calculations are carried out for the volume of caught water.

In most cases it is impossible to count all specimens of an abundant species in the sample. In this case it is recommended to conduct relative counting. The whole sample is poured into a measuring glass (graduated cylinder); water is then added to the sample in order to receive a desired volume (for instance, 100 ml). A small volume of water with organism is then taken using a pipette. The pipette contents are poured into a counting chamber. Specimens are counted only in the part of the collected sample.

For instance, let us assume that the volume of the sample is diluted with water up to 100 ml, then 5 pipettes of 5 ml of the sample are taken (i.e. 25 ml); thus specimens will be counted in the ¼ of the sample volume. Water in a measuring glass should be stirred up each time before inserting a pipette in order to draw water.

Using this procedure, data on the number of abundant species will be obtained for each sampling site and each date during the season. It is recommended to visualize changes of numbers of species in the form of graphs.

Options to use procedures

Objectives of zooplankton studies and options of zooplankton investigations can be rather diverse. Interesting pictorial data can be obtained in the course of comparison of species composition in similar polluted and clear water bodies. For instance, if there are similar ponds of about the same size, and one of them is located close to a large factory, then it is possible to reveal the implications of chemical contamination by studying species composition and population dynamics of some species. It is not obvious that numbers of animals in the water body which is subject to pollution will be lower than numbers of living organisms in the clear water body. However, species composition found in the polluted water body is almost always depleted. Only some species, which are adapted to survival under **unfavorable conditions** are usually found in polluted water. However, number of species is a characteristic of a certain water body and you cannot conclude that if there are only 25 species found in the water body then it is depleted and if there are 50 species, it is rich in species. Any conclusions can be drawn only on the basis of comparison of similar water bodies.

Under **normal conditions** the following species are abundant in open waters of lakes and water bodies: among Cladocera species: large Daphnia species (D.galeata, D.lonyispina, D.hyalina) and large Bosmina (B.coregoni, B.longis pina). In the case of smaller organisms predominate in plankton, one can assume that there are many fish in the lake and young fish feed mainly on relatively large plankton organisms. Comparing data on dominant species in different years, one can reveal trends to increase or decline in fish populations in the water body.

Other factors can also influence changes in **dominant species**. For instance, there is a recent trend that many lakes are more intensively overgrown in summer, i.e. an enormous number of unicellular and colonial algae develop in summer. It is associated with what is called "**anthropogeneous eutrophication,**" i.e. an increase in the content of mineral salts and organic compounds necessary for algae development in the water body, which are due to fertilizer wash-out from fields and discharge of organic wastewater, etc. Different animals withstand "*florification*" differently; some of them are suppressed by it, others grow in number. It can also cause changes in the dominant species in the water body. In this case, some species will predominate in the middle of summer, whereas other species will prevail in spring and at the beginning of summer as well as at the end of summer and in autumn.

Study of fauna of temporary water bodies

This manual describes the procedure for studying vernal pools in spring. Students analyze the species composition of animals found in temporary water bodies at different distances away from a constant water reservoir. A general plan for the organization of studies is given, as well as a technique for sampling (catching animals), processing, and representation of data.

Introduction

In the course of the research, the objects under study are so-called **temporary water bodies**, i.e. water reservoirs that fill up with water for a short time and that dry out quickly. The lifetime of temporary water bodies is different: from several days up to several months. Temporary water bodies also differ in their origin.

Temporary water bodies found in the *temperate climatic zone* are usually formed in spring – during a period of snowmelt and spring river floods (spring tide). In the central part of Russia, this period usually takes place at the end of April to the beginning of May. Temporary water bodies can also appear in other seasons, for instance, after heavy rainfalls in summer and following river floods (freshets). However, due to the regulated streams of most plain rivers (the presence of dams and water-storage reservoirs), summer floods and, correspondingly, temporary water bodies have become quite rare.

Temporary water bodies are quite common in other climatic zones of the earth as well, and not only in spring. They are formed in the well-known rainy season in Africa, Asia, and South America: at low latitudes, where monsoons and trade winds dominate.

Many animals have **adapted to life in temporary water bodies**, both invertebrates and vertebrates. Among vertebrates they are, first of all, amphibians. They are active when water is available, but when the water body dries up they migrate to the nearest constant water reservoirs (in the example of frogs) or they fall into *anabiosis* until the next time the temporary water body is filled (for example, tritons).

However, **invertebrate** animals constitute the largest part of the animal community in temporary water bodies. They will be objects of the given research as well. Most invertebrates that find habitat in temporary water bodies are arthropods (mainly, crustaceans and insects) and mollusks. Some of them migrate upon sensing unfavorable conditions for their existence (*flying insects*), others survive drought by burying into silt (*crustaceans* and *mollusks*).

This research will help us to find out what animals inhabit temporary water bodies, what adaptations animals have for survival under unfavorable conditions, and how do these adaptations realize.

The following **equipment,** which is standard for *hydrobiological* studies, is required for these studies: scrapers, sieves, nets, i.e. devices designed for catching invertebrates, white dishes (basins) to sort out caught animals under field conditions, cans with covers to transport samples, field diaries, field guides and binoculars.

General plan of the organization of studies

This research is aimed at study of animal populations of different types in temporary water-bodies of your area. Hence, the **objectives** of the study are: 1.) The search for temporary water bodies that can be found in this season in the vicinity of the school or field studies center; 2.) Classification of available temporary water bodies according to their origin type (feeding) and distance from the main constant body of water; 3.) Sampling (i.e. catching) of invertebrate animals in each type of the found temporary water bodies; 4) Determination of caught animals; 5) Compiling lists of animal species according to types of temporary water bodies; 6) Analysis of the dependence of animal species composition on the type of temporary water body.

Choice of objects under study

Temporary water bodies serve as the objects under study in the course of this research. As it has been said in the introduction, they are water bodies that exist for a short period of time and are formed as a result of snow melting or a river flood. Accordingly, the most typical existing temporary water bodies under conditions existing in the central part of Russia can be divided into two or three groups.

First, there are puddles (ponds and lakelets), which are formed within the river or stream **floodplain** or close to a lake or pond, due to spring flood of the main water body. Size and depth of such water bodies are of no principal importance for conducting the studies; the most important thing is that the water body is temporary and that waters of the main water reservoir formed it.

The second type includes puddles formed as the result of **snowmelt**.

Location of such puddles (near a river or a water body, or far away from it) as well as the size of puddles are of no significance. It is important that the puddle is filled with snowmelt water.

The third type of temporary water bodies includes puddles formed in **ruts** of country (forest, field) roads, which are very common in the central part of Russia. These puddles can be regarded as a separate type only conventionally, as they are filled up with water from snowmelt in spring. However, from a *biocenosis* point of view, these puddles differ from puddles filled up with snowmelt water as they remain for most of the year, as a rule, but they can dry up in summer. These puddles are mainly filled with rain for most of the year. Correspondingly, in theory, the animal community found in such puddles should differ from animal composition found in puddles formed as the result of snowmelt. In the context of the course of this research, it is recommended to distinguish these water bodies as a separate type and to examine whether they differ in species composition from snow puddles.

Prior to the fieldwork, a **reconnaissance survey** should be carried out within the area in order to determine what types of temporary water bodies can be found in the vicinity of the school and how many such water bodies there are. If there are few temporary water bodies, then students can limit themselves to the study of one or two water bodies of each type. If there are many of them, then the studies can be made comprehensive, and students will analyze the species composition of animals not only according to the origin types of water bodies, but also according to their **distance** away from the main water reservoir in the given area.

This research can turn out to be quite interesting from the point of view of revealing the **causes of the specific composition** of animals in different water bodies. The fact is that as experience shows, temperate water bodies are somehow connected with the main water bodies in the given area, even if they are located at a far distance away from them, and their waters cannot be mixed. As animals found in temporary water bodies migrate for large distances (*amphibians* or *flying insects*), so the composition of animal populations in the temporary water body always depends on the nearest large constant water reservoir. To determine whether this is correct and that in general, the species composition of animals inhabiting temporary water bodies depends on the distance from the constant water reservoir, that is what this part of the study will help you to find out.

So, different types of water bodies, according to their **origin** (type of feeding) and **distance** away from the main constant water reservoir are distinguished within the area under study before the beginning of the field studies. It is obvious that riverside puddles cannot be found far away from the river, so it is possible to include in the comparative studies, for instance, the following types of temporary water bodies: 1.) three types of puddles, located not far from the river: formed by the river, formed by snow and found in road ruts; 2.) several types of snow puddles, located not far from the river (up to 1km) and far from the river (3-4km); 3.) several types of road-rut puddles (which are also found near the river, not far from the river and far away from it).

Thus, seven temporary water bodies will be studied in the course of this research.

Conducting the field part of the work depends on availability of equipment for the collection of animals and the number of students.

It is more efficient to send one team of students (2-4 people) with a complete set of equipment to the river in order to "catch through" the riverside puddles (*river-formed, snow,* and *"road"*) and another team should be sent to the remote sites to catch animals in snow and "road" puddles at average and large distances from the river.

Fieldwork

Sampling

Sampling in *hydrobiology* is the collection of objects under study (in our case, invertebrates) with the help of some standard tools and in compliance with a standard procedure. Compliance with **standards** is important, just as in any other scientific research. If, for instance, sampling in one water body will be carried out with the help of a net on a long handle with a bag made of fine-meshed kapron, and in another water body, with the help of a manual sieve (colander), the results will obviously differ. It is also important to comply with standards for choosing the part of the water body where collection will take place: if animals are caught with a net by dragging the net on the bottom, then in other water bodies, students cannot catch animals in the water column. And so on.

The main tool for catching aquatic invertebrates is a scraper, which is a metal frame with a cutting edge, where a bag made of tight cotton fabric and fine-meshed kapron is attached. The frame is fixed on a stick (Fig. 1):

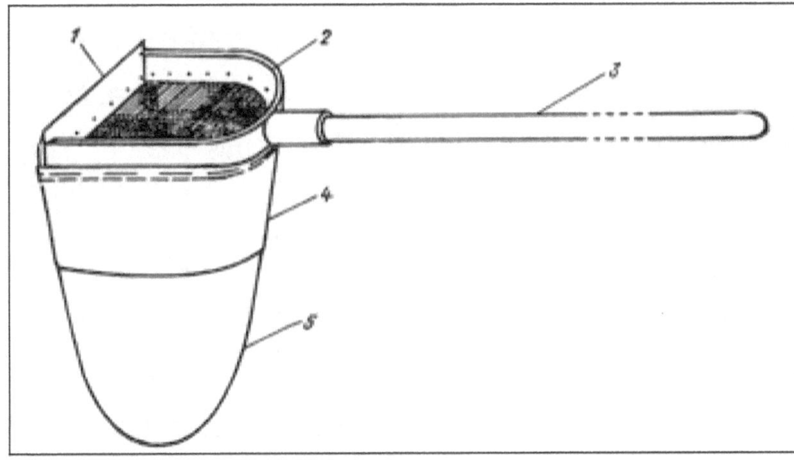

Figure 1: Scraper: 1 – cutting edge; 2 – frame; 3 – handle; 4 – cotton fabric part of the washing sieve; 5 – part of the sieve made of kapron.

As it is shown in Figure 1, kapron is not sewn directly to the metal frame but through a cotton strip. Thus, it is possible to extend the "life" of the kapron bag, because if it is sewn directly to the metal it will soon be torn.

The scraper is the most universal tool of all standard catching devices used in hydrobiology. The scraper allows the student investigator to collect both qualitative and quantitative samples from all types of substrates, including such specific substrates as the submerged overgrown sides of ferries, walls of hydro-engineering facilities, the piles of bridges and so on.

The procedure for sampling has its own peculiarities in each of the natural substrata.

When collecting samples in the river, the scraper should first be

placed **downstream,** regarding the substrate from which the samples are to be collected. In this case, organisms will fall into the scraper's screen with the water current, together with suspended soil particles or substrate fragments. In fast rivers, use a foot to stir up the bottom; a person should move with one side forward and place the scraper facing downstream On **rocky substrates,** the organisms should first be washed into the scrape from the rock surface with a gentle movement of one's hand, then the scraper should be turned upside down, and it should smooth the bottom surface. When a large cluster of algae or macrophytes fall into the scraper, they should be shaken in the water without taking them out of the screen, and then removed. Large pebbles that fall into the screen should be removed after the screen is carefully examined and all organisms are taken out with the help of tweezers (forceps).

When samples are collected from separate specimens or thinned out thickets of **plants and filamentous algae**, they should be shaken in the screen of the scraper, submerged into the water, and then they should be once again examined in order to collect attached organisms. When collecting samples from dense thickets of *microphytes*, the scraper should be merged into the thicket and then thickets should be "mowed" with sharp, energetic movements.

Temporary water bodies are specific concerning their **bottom structure**. The bottom of a puddle is often covered with leaves, branches and twigs; road ruts are often quite narrow. Catching invertebrates in such places should be carried out carefully, as large objects should be accurately taken out of the water and they should be closely examined prior to throwing them away.

Depending on the size of the water body, structure and littering of its bottom, students can also use an entomological net or even a simple fine-meshed plastic sieve in addition to the scraper in the course of collecting in the temporary water bodies (Fig.2: Entomological net).

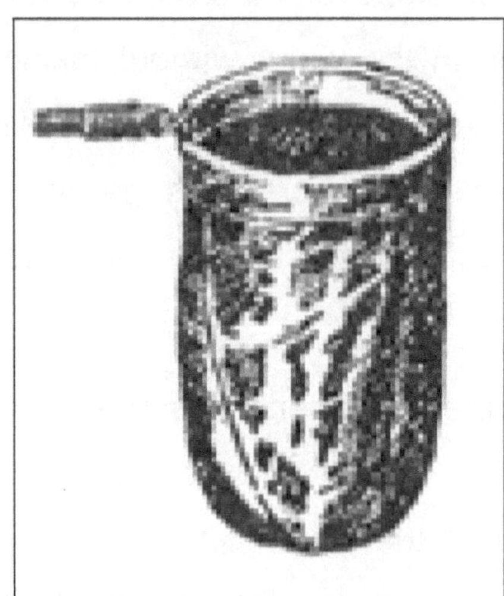

As it has been said, the most important point is that different types of water bodies undergo sampling with the help of the same tools.

After each collection of samples, the scraper should be taken out of water and its contents should be carefully put into a cuvette (container) or a dishpan filled with clean water from the river. The screen should be turned inside out. All organisms seen by the naked eye should be collected (with fingers, or with the help of pincers (forceps), spoon, etc., depending on the size) and placed into a glass container with a wide neck for sample storage and transportation to the field center. Due to their active movements even small organisms are easily seen in a white cuvette.

All animals caught in different temporary water bodies (according to the above-planned classification) can be put in one container (glass jar).

Accompanying descriptions of water bodies

Before starting to collect benthos samples, the riverside zone should be examined. All soils should be observed about 50 meters upstream and 50 meters down. Directly at the sampling site the typical appearance of the riverside zone should be recorded and a map of the area sketched. In addition, the student researchers should record: 1) number of the sample; 2) date and time of sampling, 3) type of the water body according to the planned classification, 4) location of sampling site (map).

The following information should also be provided: 1) water and air temperature at the time of sample collection, 2) weather conditions on the day of sampling. It is advisable to record a visual description of the hydrological parameters of the water body in the field diary: 1) stream velocity, 2) water color, 3) water smell, and 4) water transparency.

Description of the water bodies ends with information on the presence of vertebrates within it (frogs, tritons, fish, etc.), frog "eggs", as well as additional data, such as if insects fly out of it, the presence of dead fish, empty shells of mollusks, litter, etc.

Laboratory processing

All samples collected under field conditions are brought to the field studies center, where students sort out and determine the caught animals in the lab. Species composition of animals is, of course, determined separately for each type of temporary water bodies (each team of students carries out sorting and determination of animals on its own).

After returning to the lab, the samples from the glass containers are poured out into white cuvettes filled with, preferably, water from the same water body (so two or three liters of water should be brought from the trip in a bottle).

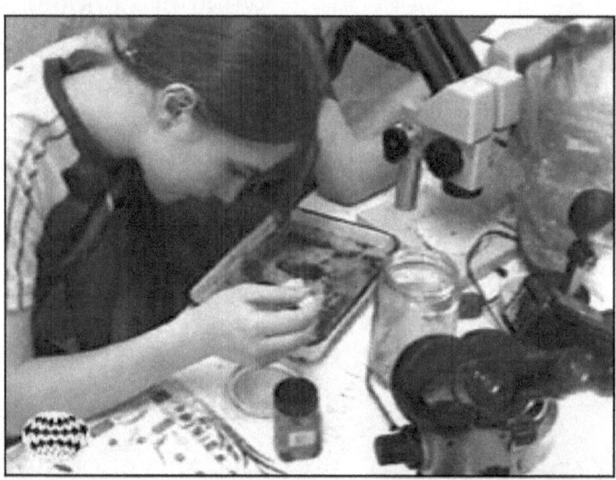

Then all collected organisms are sorted into Petri dishes. Organisms of the same species (at least according to their appearance) are placed in one dish.

Then collected animals are determined according to guide tables, if necessary using a binocular microscope. It is advisable that each student gets training in species determination and draws at least one organism.

When the determination of animals is over, a summarized list of caught animals is compiled for each type of temporary water body. It is recommended to present it in the form of the following table (Table 1, an example):

Number of species	Types of temporary water bodies						
	"River side" puddl es	Snow puddles **near** the river	Snow puddles **not far from** the river	Snow puddles **far from** the river	"Road" puddles **near** the river	"Road" puddles **not far from** the river	"Road" puddles **far from** the river
Insects	5	2	3	2	2	4	5
Crustaceans	6	3	1	0	5	3	1
Mollusks	4	1	0	0	0	0	0
Other species	4	3	1	2	5	3	3

The obtained data can be visually presented in the form of graphs or diagrams:

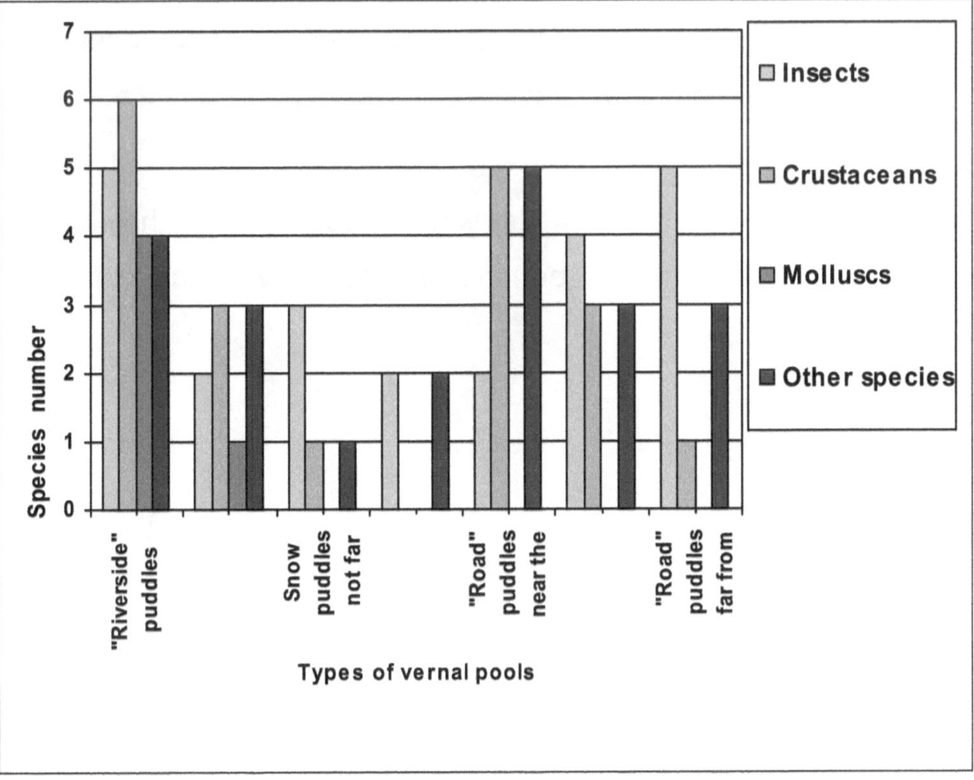

Figure 3. Example of diagram plotting on the degree different animal groups are representative in different types of water bodies (based on data of Table 1)

Analyzing the obtained data, students should try to answer **the following questions**:

1. Does the species composition of animals vary in different water bodies, which differ in origin (type of feeding) and distance away from the constant water body?

2. Which water bodies have the highest numbers of animals and which have the least, and why?

3. What animals prevail in specific types of water bodies and why?

4. How does the species composition of animals change depending on the distance from the river (within water bodies fed the same way)?

5. Judging on the found animals, what adaptations do they use for survival during unfavorable periods of temporary drying out of the water body?

Studies of species composition and abundance of amphibians

This manual contains a procedure for the organization of studies of the numbers and population structure of amphibians in spring and summer. The method of selecting habitats for study, the technique for a route census of frogs, the procedure for the simplest measurements of caught animals and the analysis of the age structure of frog populations found in different biotopes are described.

Introduction

If we look at the history and culture of humankind, amphibians as well as reptiles have always aroused a feeling of suspicious interest and some superstitious fear. In fairy tales and legends of many peoples of the world, they were the prototypes of dark forces, evil and danger. Despite all of these superstitions, amphibians are very sensitive, interesting and unusual animals.

Amphibia is the first and most primitive class of terrestrial vertebrates. Their fish-like progenitors appeared on Earth in the Devonian period (about 350 million years ago). In spite of long-term evolution, amphibians kept a number of primitive features, which they inherited from their ancestors.

Most modern amphibians (which are divided into three orders – **Apoda**, **Caudata** and **Anura**, with a total of 4500 species) are closely connected to life in the course of their **life cycle**. They deposit their spawn (eggs) in water, where development of embryos and larvae takes place. Mature amphibians (most species) spend most of their life on land. Such a "double" life, i.e. life in two types of habitats, **aquatic** and **terrestrial**, is reflected in the Latin name of these animals (*Amphibia*). Unlike other vertebrates, the skin of Amphibia is smooth – there are no scales, feathers or hair; it is often moist to touch due to numerous glands.

A diversity of amphibians is not found in the northern and temperate climatic zones of the Earth (most of them are found in the lower, tropical latitudes). Thus, a number of species found in a specific area does not exceed five to eight for the majority of the Russian territory. The reason for this is the **poikilothermy** of amphibians, i.e. the inconstancy of their body temperature, which greatly depends on the temperature of their environment. The cold climate of temperate and northern latitudes results in the fact that not many amphibian species can exist there. That is why it is so interesting to study amphibians under severe conditions that are almost unsuitable for the existence of cold-blooded animals. In addition, the low species diversity of amphibians makes the educational study of these species easier. Besides, these species are not as active and cautious as other invertebrates, and they can be caught easily in order to examine them more closely: to measure and weigh them. All these factors greatly contribute to the possibilities of their study by students.

The study is aimed at an **amphibian census** carried out within the vicinities of the school or field studies center. Students catch amphibians and analyze the size and age structure of their populations in different biotopes of the surrounding area in the course of conducting the studies. The most favorable period for the given study is the end of spring and the beginning of summer, i.e. the period of highest activity for amphibians, their breeding and migrations.

Students will use the following equipment in the course of their studies: containers for catching frogs (buckets), rulers (slide gauge) for measurements, a laboratory balance, field diaries and calculators.

Preparation for carrying out the study

At the preparation stage, students should learn about the expected composition of amphibian species within the specific area and proposed procedures for studies. In order to do this, it is necessary to make a **list of amphibian species** in the area using available atlases, manuals and field guides. Students should also recollect the general rules for route census, which were taught in previous lessons of the given series: census of fungi ("Study of Species Composition and Number of Fungi", Part 2: Botany) and bird census ("Study of Species Composition and Census of Birds Using the Line Transect-counting Method", Part 3: Zoology).

As the research is aimed at studying the **species composition**, numbers and age structure of amphibian populations **in different biotopes**, so it is recommended to begin by making a list of biotopes under study – as it is done during all studies within the given series on carrying out research on the habitat variability of specific indicators.

If this short-term research (1-2 days) is carried out by a small group of students (10-15 people), then it is recommended to include four or five biotopes (habitats) in the list of habitats for studies and for subsequent comparison, which contrast the most (from the amphibians' point of view). For this purpose it is the most interesting to analyze the differences in amphibian populations according to two parameters: distance from the main water body where they breed, and degree of habitat aridity (moisture). The following scheme of studies can be proposed as an example.

The census should first be carried out in two biotopes in the immediate vicinity of the water-body (a *river, lake,* or *pond*): in an open area and in the forest (open bank and a bank overgrown with forest or shrubbery).

Second, the census should be conducted in two or three biotopes at an average distance from the water body. They can include clearings in the *forest* or *fields*, as well as different forest types at a distance of 500-1000 m from a body of water.

The third group of biotopes will include the same habitats but at a considerable distance from the water body (3-5km).

Thus, different types of habitats will be studied and later compared; similar studies will be carried out in each of the biotopes and obtained data will be compared.

Before the field studies, all students are divided into work teams (teams include two or three students) according to the number of bodies of water under study (or at least, groups of biotopes, for instance, close to the water body, not far and far from the water body). Each team goes to a specified biotope with a map of the area, field diaries and containers designed for catching frogs (buckets).

Fieldwork

Technique of the route census

The simplest and easiest method for students to take a census of amphibians is with a **route census** within a band of a certain width. The route is a line (straight or slightly curved), which crosses the biotope or goes along a bank of the water body. The student who conducts the census goes along the route and registers (counts and records in the field diary) all frogs seen within a band of a certain width. All animals found **outside the census band are not registered**.

The width of the band covered by one student depends on **features of the habitat** and on the possibilities to detect animals within the band. If the area is open and it is well looked through, the width of the band can be made wider, if the habitat is overgrown with shrubbery or high grass (coastal vegetation), the band can be made narrower.

On average, experience of such studies shows that a student can notice frogs with certainty within the band that is 4-10m wide (2-5

meters on each side of the route). If several students carry out the census, then it can be carried out in a "chain," and total width of the census band will be larger and census data will be more reliable.

Hence, before the census, it is necessary to plan a model route for students' movement across the chosen biotope. If the census is carried out along the bank of a water body, then the first student goes right along the water line, the second, at a distance of five meters away from the water line. It is not recommended to carry out the census farther from the water line, as it is better to conduct the census much further (100 meters and more) away from the water body. In this case the habitat should be distinguished as a separate biotope. When the census is carried out in habitats located far from the water body, then the total width of the band can be made larger and the census should be carried out in "a chain," i.e. by several students.

When the census is carried out by a group of students, then each student conducts his or her own census, i.e. registers all frogs found **within the bounds of one's own band** in his or her own field diary. In order to avoid double census of the same animals, students who move in a chain should coordinate their actions with each other: they go in one line and do not go ahead or behind the group. In addition, they should decide which person records "arguable" frogs found in the area within the boundary between two students' bands.

If several species of frogs are present in the area under study, then they should be visually **determined** in the course of the census. If the species are well distinguished from each other, then census of each species should be conducted separately. If the species cannot be visually distinguished from afar, their determination should be carried out later in the laboratory on the basis of the analysis of frogs caught for measurements (see below).

Length of the census route depends on two factors: the total width of the census band and the number of frogs. The wider the band is and the more abundant the frogs are, then the route length can be made shorter. Experience from similar censuses shows that reliable data can be obtained when the census band is 10-15 meters wide and route length is about 500-600 meters, and if numbers of animals are quite high, over 50-60 animals are registered in the course of the census.

Records in the field diary are made in a line by the "accumulation" method according to the **"library"** system: . - 1, .. - 2, :. - 3, :: -4, ⁙ - 5, ⁙ - 6, ⊔ - 7, ⊓ - 8, ⊠ - 9, ⊠ -10, — similar to record-keeping for mushroom census, birds, tracks, etc. In addition to the number of found frogs, the following information is written down in the field diary: general information on the habitat, where the census takes place, and the conditions of the census (date, administrative and geographical location of the habitat, name and brief description of the biotope, weather conditions in the course of census period, authors of the census).

The necessary condition for conducting the census is measuring the distance covered by the census (it is easiest to do this by counting steps or according to the map of the area), as well as the exact width of the census band. This data will be used in the estimation of the population density of frogs and it should also be recorded in the field diary when the census is over.

Catching frogs

As the present research is aimed not only at a quantitative census of frogs but also at studying the age structure of frog populations, **catching** frogs is one the components of fieldwork. It is more efficient to organize the catching of frogs for subsequent laboratory measurements simultaneously with the route census.

The simplest catching technique is to catch all frogs met within the

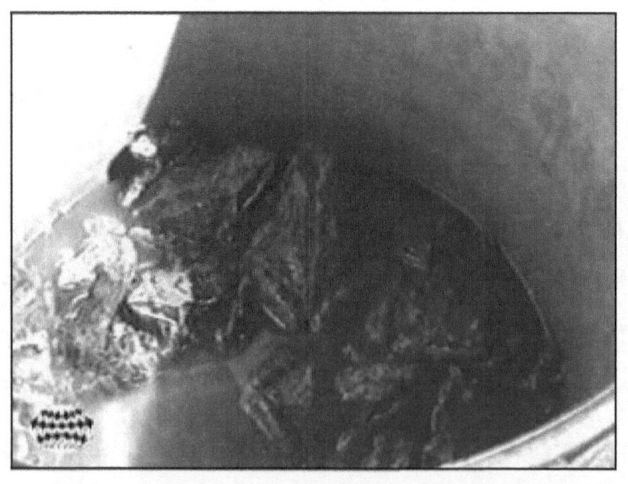

census band and to place all the frogs into a bucket with a cover (the bucket should be filled with 2-3cm of water taken from the nearest body of water).

Frogs are caught **by hand** or with a small net. Hand catching requires adroitness and specific skills, but it turns out to be more efficient in the end result, and it also gives many merry minutes of activity (even professionals catch frogs by hand!). It is not easy to do while conducting a census along the banks of the water body – as a rule the frogs, which have been frightened away, jump right into the water. If students use a net, they can try to catch frogs in the water. If there is no net, then they will use only those frogs that the students managed to "separate" from the water and catch ashore.

It is enough to catch 50-60 frogs in each of the biotopes under study in order to carry out the full-value research of the age structure of frog populations. Hence, there is no need to catch frogs along the whole census route if the density of frogs is quite high in the course of the census.

Frogs should not be caught selectively, for instance, the largest and the least active. In this case, data on population structure will be incorrect. All frogs should be caught in the course of the census, regardless of their size and activity.

When census and catching is over, all caught frogs are brought to the camp (field center) in buckets.

Laboratory measurements and calculations

Calculations of population density

Calculations of population density are carried out for each of the studied biotope routes. The procedure is quite simple: first it is necessary to estimate the area of the studied site: this is the width of the census route multiplied by the route length. If several students carried out the census, then the total width of the census band is taken into account.

All frogs encountered in the course of the census (and registered in the field diary) are referred to a standard unit of area – hectare or a square kilometer.

Example: three students registered correspondingly 58, 32, and 62 frogs in the course of the census, with a route length of 500 meters. Each student carried out a census within the band of four meters wide (two meters to each side of the route line). Thus, the studied area amounted (4m x 3) x 500 = 6,000 square meters. Converted to hectares, the area amounted to 0.6 ha (1 ha = 100 x 100m or 10,000 square meters). The total number of frogs found was 58+32+62 = 152 specimens. So we can calculate the density of frogs per 1 ha (1/0.6) x 152 = 253 specimens per ha. So then it is easy to calculate density per 1 square km: 253 x 100 (100 ha in 1 square km) = 25,300 specimens per square km.

Measurements

All caught frogs are measured in the laboratory and, if possible, weighed. In principle, if there is no scale or time available, it is possible to limit the data to measurements; it is quite enough to determine age classes of frogs. Weighing is an alternative method to determine the age of frogs, but the data can provide additional useful information on state of frog populations. In other words, if time and a scale are available, then weighing can be carried out; if not, students can just measure the size of caught frogs.

Measurements are conducted according to the scheme that is standard for amphibians: using a ruler or slide gauge, students measure the length of each frog's body from the muzzle tip to the *cloaca* hole (Figure 1).

Measurements are taken along the abdominal side of the animal. It is easier to measure live frogs by holding them in your hand. They calm down, as a rule, when turned on their back, and will let the students measure them.

It is more convenient for two students to measure a frog: one takes measurements and another writes them down. Three students can do it together as well: one holds the frog, the second takes measurements and the third writes them down.

Measurement data is recorded in a simple table according to size groups (classes). Size classes are chosen at will, on the basis of minimal and maximal sizes. For instance, the smallest caught frog was 12mm long and the largest one measured 120mm. It is recommended to divide all frogs at the initial stage into 10-12 classes – each 8-10 mm form one class; so all records are written in the form of a table:

Size, mm	Number of frogs	Size, mm	Number of frogs	Size, mm	Number of frogs
12-22		53-62		93-102	
23-32		63-72		103-112	
33-42		73-82		113-122	
43-52		83-92			

The number of frogs of the specific size class is recorded similarly to the procedure of record keeping in the course of the census: according to a "library" method.

Of course, measurements are carried out separately for each biotope

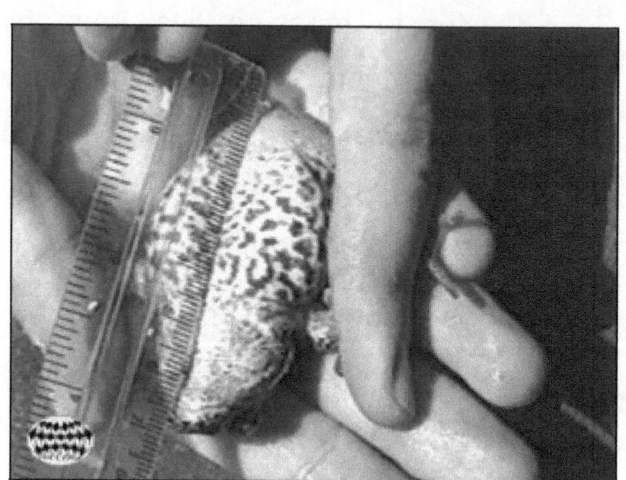

group of frogs. i.e. each group of students measures its "own" frogs that have been caught in the same biotope. Thus, separate tables of measurement data are made for each of the biotopes.

If weighing is also carried out, then the weight data is also recorded in a similar table or in the same table as well. The scheme of determining weight classes is similar: the smallest and the largest frogs are weighed, and then the whole range of weights is divided into about 10 classes.

Determining the age classes

Then evaluation of the age structure of frog populations in different biotopes is carried out on the basis of measurements taken.

The principles for determining age classes is based on the fact that frogs breed once a year and grow for approximately the same value during a year, regardless of the habitat (size and weight increase about one and a half to two times during the year). Correspondingly, if several size classes (groups, gradations) are distinguished within the frog population, then it is more likely that the classes will correspond with different ages of animals with an interval of one year.

Calculations include two stages. The first stage is revealing the true size classes of frogs. Dividing all the frogs into 10 classes in the course of taking measurements was artificial and arbitrary. It is more likely that all frogs will be divided into two, three, or four size-and-age classes at closer examination. The class comprising the smallest sized frogs is composed of frogs born in the current or last year (depending on the season of studies), the following size class consists of frogs that are a year older and so on.

Creating age classes is, of course, subjective, but experience of similar studies shows that, as a rule, the ages of frogs (with an interval of one year) are well distinguished on the basis of the frogs' measurement data.

However, there are more objective methods to determine age classes with the help of statistical methods, but students can do without statistics in the course of these studies. They should just examine the table and find out which size groups (among 10-12 distinguished classes) have more in common with each other than with other classes. Let us illustrate this idea with an example.

Let us assume that we obtained the following table as the result of measurements:

Size, mm	Number of frogs	Size, mm	Number of frogs	Size, mm	Number of frogs
12-22	23	53-62	16	93-102	5
23-32	11	63-72	3	103-112	9
33-42	2	73-82	2	113-122	2
43-52	9	83-92	1		

With a close look at the data it is obvious that all frogs can be roughly divided into three groups of the following sizes: 12-32mm (the first age class), 43-62mm (the second class) and 93-112mm (the third class). All frogs belonging to "transition" groups are referred to the nearest maximums or they are simply ignored (they are excluded from the following processing).

Thus, the following distribution of frogs according to "age" classes is obtained. We write the word "age" in quotation marks as we have indirect data on the age of frogs (we did not measure their age). Thus, we receive the following table of age classes:

Age classes	Number of frogs
The first age class (12-32mm)	34
The second age class (43-62mm)	25
The third age class (93-112mm)	14

Diagrams can be plotted on the basis of obtained data and biotopes can be compared (Figure 2). The diagrams can indicate both an absolute number of frogs caught in a specific biotope and percentage ratio of frogs of different ages. If the areas studied in each of the biotopes differed in size, then it is better to plot the percentage of frogs on the diagrams and not the absolute number of caught animals.

It makes more sense visually to mark the data on density of frogs belonging to different age classes in different biotopes on the diagram. If only some of the frogs were caught in the course of census then first it is necessary to estimate the total density of frogs within the specific biotope. Then, after measurements are over, it is necessary to calculate how many frogs of a specific age are found in the sample. Then students should calculate the percentage ratio of frogs belonging to different age classes in the given biotope. At the final stage, they should estimate what share of the frog population density a certain age class of frogs makes up. This data can be plotted on the diagram.

Using this method of data representation, it is possible to show not only the age structure of frog populations in different biotopes, but also numbers of frogs: both the total and the number of frogs belonging to different age classes (Figure 2).

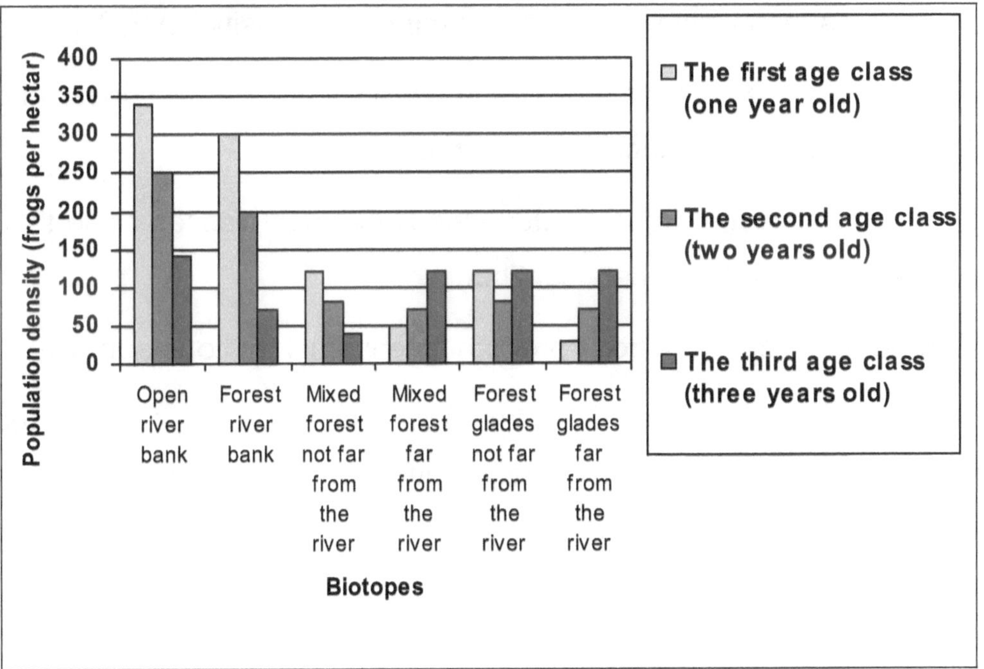

Figure 2. Model diagram of the age structure of frog populations found in different biotopes

Analyzing the given example, it is noticeable that younger (one-year-old) frogs prevail over old ones in areas located closer to the river. At an average distance from the water body, their ratio is almost equal, whereas old (three-year-old) frogs prevail over younger ones far from the water body. At the same time, the total number of frogs decreases according to the distance away from the water body and the share of old frogs is higher in open biotopes.

Analyzing the obtained data in a similar way, students should answer the following questions:

1) What biotopes are characterized by the maximum density of frog populations, and which ones with the minimum density? Why?

2) Does the density of frogs change in different biotopes and depending on the distance from the water body?

3) Are all the caught frogs divided clearly into age classes or do their sizes change gradually as a continuum?

4) What age classes of frogs predominate in each biotope and why?

5) Does the age structure of the frog population depend on the structure of the biotope and distance away from the water body, and what factor among the listed ones has the largest influence on the age structure?